Can You Top This?
Yes!

And here is the greatest collection of comics ever gathered together in one book to do just that!

Morey Amsterdam	Nipsy Russell
Shelly Berman	Merv Griffin
Bob Newhart	Soupy Sales
Phyllis Diller	Henny Youngman
Steve Allen	Jo Anne Worley
Rose Marie	Red Buttons
George Burns	Jack Carter
Mickey Rooney	George Gobel
Danny Thomas	Dick Gautier
Paul Winchell	Jim Backus
Arte Johnson	Jerry Van Dyke
Pat O'Brien	Louis Nye
Jan Murray	Stu Gilliam
Jackie Vernon	Alan Sues
George Kirby	Jessie White
Vincent Price	Sammy Shore
Ernest Borgnine	Richard Dawson
Milton Berle	Laurence Harvey
Bob Crane	Bill Dana
Caesar Romero	Monte Hall

CAN YOU TOP THIS?

by
**THE PANELISTS AND GUEST STARS
OF THE SHOW**

BOOKS

GROSSET & DUNLAP, INC.
A NATIONAL GENERAL COMPANY
New York

Contents

CAN YOU TOP THIS?

1

Shaggy Dogs and Their Friends

Some people like the ballet
And dance upon their toes.
I'd rather be an elephant
And squirt water through my nose.

A mother cat, followed by her three little kittens, was quietly walking down the street. Suddenly from around the corner a ferocious dog charged at her and her kittens. Shooing the kittens ahead of her, she backed down the street and into an alley. It was a dead end. There was no way to escape. The mother cat could think of only one thing to do. She stared at the dog and said, "Woof, woof, woof." The dog was so startled that he turned and ran. The mother cat turned to her kittens and said, "Now you can appreciate the value of a second language."

He was a hippie—disheveled, with a beard that looked messy, like if you hit it, moths would fly out. And he had very long hair. He was walking along the street with a pig under his arm. Another hippie came up to him and said, "Hey, man, that pig—where'd you get it?" And the pig looked up and said, "I bought him at an auction."

Two flies met on the street, and one fly said, "Mrs. Buzz-buzz, you look tired. What's the matter?" "Oh, I had a dreadful night, the baby was sick, and I had to walk the ceiling all night with him."

The canary limped home and into his cage. The other canary said:

"What happened to you?"

"I got caught in a badminton game."

Business was slow at the moment and the bartender was wiping the glasses and generally cleaning up. The door opened and a gorilla walked in. He came up to the bar and sat down on a stool. The bartender went over and the gorilla said, "I want a vodka martini, very dry, with a twist of lemon, on the rocks, please." The bartender looked at the gorilla and said, "Certainly, certainly. Here you are, sir." He put the drink in front of the gorilla and walked quickly into the back room.

"Hey, boss, there's a gorilla out there!"

"What do you mean?"

"A gorilla, a big gorilla!"

The boss opened the door a crack, looked out, and said, "It's a gorilla, all right."

"What'll I do? He asked me for a drink."

"Did you give it to him?"

"Sure. What am I supposed to do? Argue with a gorilla?"

"Okay. Charge him like anybody else. No, wait. Gorillas aren't very bright. Charge him twenty-five dollars."

"Twenty-five dollars?"

"Yeh."

The bartender went back to the bar and the gorilla said, "Very tasty. How much will that be, please?"

"That'll be twenty-five dollars."

The gorilla said, "Hmmmmmm. . . ." and reached into his pocket. The bartender kept staring at him. The gorilla said, "What are you looking at?"

"Sorry, I don't mean to offend. It's just that we don't get too many gorillas around here, you know."

The gorilla said, "And at these prices you aren't going to get many, either."

Two pigeons were flying along peacefully when suddenly a big jet plane shot right by them. One pigeon said to the other, "That big bird sure must be in a hurry." And the other pigeon answered, "You'd be in a hurry too, if your tail were on fire."

A parrot in a pet store sat on his perch, bragging to the other birds: "I'm the smartest bird in the world." "Well, if you're so smart, what can you do?" "Pull the string on my right leg and I do the Funky Chicken. Have you ever seen a parrot do the Funky Chicken?" "What about the string on your left leg?" "Pull the string on my left leg and I do the Frug and the Bugaloo." "What happens if I pull both strings?" "I fall on my fanny."

The owner of a world-famous circus received a phone call one day in his office. "Mr. North, I'm one of the greatest acts that you have ever seen. I sing like Crosby, I dance like Astaire, I tell jokes like Hope, I'm just wonderful. I do impressions, everything." North said, "So?" "Well, the first thing I have to tell you is very important—I'm a dog." "You're a what?" "I'm a dog." "Forget it," North said. "Why don't you just be yourself."

Two pigeons were flying around one day and nearly crashed. The beautiful female pigeon said, "Oh, my goodness, you nearly dented my beak." He said, "I'm sorry. As soon as I saw you, I was so taken by your beauty that I fell in love with you." "Thank you, that is quite a compliment." "Will you have lunch here with me tomorrow?" "I'll see you tomorrow." The next day he arrived with sandwiches and they had a marvelous time. Soon they were seeing each other every day. He suggested that the next day they should fly together to the waterfront to watch the ships go out. She said, "Fine. Meet me at the cathedral." The next day he was there as agreed at 11 o'clock. She wasn't there by 11:30 or even 12 o'clock. He started pacing along the parapet. A friend came by and said, "What's the matter?" "I'm very worried about my girl friend. Maybe I . . ." Just then he looked down and there she was on the sidewalk. He flew down and said, "Thank goodness you're safe. I've been so worried about you. What happened? I thought you had been in an accident." "No, it was such a lovely day that I decided to walk."

The two Italian flies were flying around the Sistine Chapel and they landed on the ceiling right on the Michelangelo painting. One fly said, "People are stupid." "What do you mean?" "Look at this beautiful ceiling—and those idiots are walking around on the floor."

A turkey showed up for football practice. He was an amazing bird—he could throw a forward pass 50 yards, fly down the field and catch it. The coach watched his performance in amazement. Finally, he went over to the bird and said, "Hey, Turk, you're sensational. You threw a 50-yard pass and then you caught it yourself. I want to sign you up. What about it? How much do you want?"

"Don't want any money," the Turk replied, shrugging his feathers.

"No money?" The coach stared at him, astounded. "What do you want then?"

"I just want to be sure the season goes past Thanksgiving."

Two rabbits wandered into one of the automobile plants in Detroit. As they stood there watching this giant assembly line with thousands of parts, one rabbit turned and looked at the other and said, "Honey, I don't want you to think I'm jealous, but they must have started with more than two."

Two lady oysters were talking. One asked the other about her date with a lobster the night before. "How was it, did you enjoy yourself?" "Oh, it was simply wonderful! First he looked deep into my eyes, and then he put his claws around me . . . oh, my God! My pearls!"

Three mice lived in a bar. When the bartender closed the place and went home, the mice came out and began running up and down the shelves. A bottle of Scotch, too close to the edge, was knocked over, fell to the floor and broke. The three mice started lapping the spilled liquor, and, in about ten minutes. . . . three blind mice. They kept staggering around. One said, "I'm going outside in the street right now, and I'm going to beat up that big cop on the corner." And the second mouse said, "Where's Muhammad Ali, also known as Cassius Clay? Let me at him! I'll rip him to shreds." The third mouse said, "The heck with that! I'm going upstairs and kiss the cat."

One day some kids were playing football outside a chicken coop and the football went right through the window into the chicken coop. The rooster looked at the football. He called the hens over and said, "I want you to see what the girls in the other coop are doing."

"Tell me, why did the elephant wear polka-dot socks?"
"I don't know. Why did the elephant wear polka-dot socks?"
"Because someone stole his tennis shoes."

"Tell me, why do elephants have hair on their tail?"
"I don't know. Why do elephants have hair on their tail?"
"Why not?"

"What did the elephant say to Sophia Loren?"
"Nothing. Elephants don't speak Italian."

"Do you know where elephants are found?"
"No, where are they found?"
"Well, they're so big, they're seldom lost . . ."

"Tell me, why do elephants lie on their back with their feet in the air?"
"I don't know. Why do they?"
"To trip birds."

Do you know what Tarzan said when he saw the elephants coming over the hill?"

"Here come the elephants over the hill."

The farmer wanted to improve his herd, so he imported this pedigreed cow from England. A year later he had still not gotten any milk from her. She had cost a lot of money, and he was getting desperate. He wrote to the Department of Agriculture for advice. They sent around a representative. The man inspected the cow and the barn, and said, "Of course she won't give any milk. You've got to clean up that barn. Cows like clean barns, and a contented cow gives milk."

So the farmer cleaned up his barn and prettied it up with new stalls and new lights and a nice paint job. Still, no milk from this cow. The farmer was angry. He walked up to the cow and said, "I've a good mind to ship you back to England. I do everything to keep you happy, but where's the milk?"

The cow said, "Yanking, pulling every night! All you want is milk! Did you ever once tell me you love me?"

Two zoologists were talking. "I've been in zoology for quite a long time and something has always baffled me. I've never been able to determine the sex of an elephant; I can't tell which are the males and which are the females." And his friend said, "Well, actually that is not very difficult at all. You just walk up to an elephant and stand on a chair. Then lift the elephant's ear. Do not breathe for at least 12 seconds. Then ask the elephant a question. Any question at all. And if she answers it, it's a female, and if he answers it, it's a male."

The animal act trainer walked into the agent's office, bubbling with enthusiasm over the new dog act he had developed. "This dog is terrific! What a mimic! The takeoffs he can do—WOW! Just let him look at any comic routine you want and he can imitate that comic—WOW, he can tell the jokes better than the comedian can." The agent listened without much interest, but agreed to see the dog perform. The dog did everything and more than his trainer had promised. The agent just sat on his hands. Exasperated the dog's trainer demanded, "So what's the matter? Isn't the dog good?" "Sure, sure—but doesn't he have any jokes of his own?"

> There was a cute little rabbit named Blink
> Who had eyes that were big, round and pink.
> He'd laugh and he'd play,
> And he'd have fun all day
> Because tomorrow he might be a mink.

A little dog walked into the library and over to the librarian and said, "Pardon me, could you show me to the section for Henry Wadsworth Longfellow?" The librarian said nothing. The dog spoke more loudly, "Dear lady, could you be so kind as to tell me whether you have any of the works of Henry Wadsworth Longfellow?" Still the librarian said nothing and just stared at the dog. Finally she spoke, "Why that's amazing." And the dog looked up and said, "Yes, I know. It is amazing. Not many people read Longfellow anymore."

The pennant race was close, and the second-place team was having trouble with its pitching. One day a horse walked over to the manager as he watched the team practice, "I hear you are looking for a good pitcher. I'm your horse. I can win the pennant for you. Why don't you try me out?" The manager figured that if the horse could talk, he could probably pitch, so he called to one of the catchers, "Go out there and warm this horse up. Let's see how he throws that ball." Everyone watched while the horse threw every kind of a ball—curve balls, fast balls, spinners that suddenly dropped. The manager called for a practice game. The horse struck out the first three men at bat. He repeated the performance in the second inning and the third. In the fourth, the horse came up to bat. The horse swung and hit. The center fielder picked up the ball, threw it to the shortstop, who threw it to the second baseman. He threw it to first and the horse was out before he made it to first. The manager called the horse over to him and said, "You pitch better than any other pitcher in the league. And you can hit. But you sure can't run." The horse said, "Do you think I'd be here if I could run?"

> A flea and a fly in a flue
> Were imprisoned, so what could they do?
>   Said the fly, "Let us flee."
>   "Let us fly," said the flea.
> So they flew through a flaw in the flue.

The old bull was being retired, being put out to pasture by the farmer. The farmer was a very kindly man. He explained to the bull, "Listen, I'm not going to sell you or kill you. I'm going to put you out in the pasture with the cows, and you can just stay there." The bull was grateful, "Thank you very much." As soon as the old bull saw the frisky young bull, he started snorting and pawing the ground and acting as if he were going to charge at the young one. "Hey, you don't have to do that," the farmer protested. "You're a little too old for such shenanigans." The old bull said, "I know. I just want that new one to know I'm not one of the cows."

A real loser in show biz figured that if he couldn't be in the acting part of it, at least he could be a producer. He collected a lot of fleas and trained them marvelously. Audiences that came to see them perform loved it. And big things started happening. The man was happy: he owned and directed the biggest flea circus of all time and he was ready to present it at the Palace. On opening night, the curtain rose and the spotlight hit center stage. He walked out: "Ladies and gentlemen, there will be no show tonight. My little flea circus just ran off with a cocker spaniel."

A hunter shot a duck, and it fell into the lake. Quickly, he commanded his dog—a dog he had never worked before —to retrieve. The hound ran to the edge of the water, sniffed . . . and walked out onto the waters of the lake. The hunter was amazed. He shot another duck; it too fell into the lake. Again the hound walked out on the water to retrieve the duck before it sank. At last, the hunter thought, he had something to show that friend of his who never let anything get to him. The next day the hunter suggested to his friend that they go do a little duck shooting. His friend shot a duck, and it fell into the lake. The dog walked across the water to retrieve it and drop it at the shooter's feet.

The hunter asked his friend, "What do you think of my bird dog?"

"Well . . ."

"Didn't you notice anything special about the dog?"

"I noticed one thing. He can't swim."

A drunk walking down the street stopped to pat a horse pulling a milk wagon. Very politely, the horse said, "Thank you. How are you?" The drunk was amazed, "But you're a horse and you're talking." "That's right, and not only do I talk, but I've had quite a life. Would you believe I once won the Kentucky Derby?" "I'll be darned. That's really something." About that time the milkman came out and the drunk ran up to him, saying, "Your horse is talking!" And the milkman said, "Of course, and I suppose he gave you that baloney about the Kentucky Derby."

The owner of a flea circus was leaving his hotel to put on a show. He was recognized and a crowd gathered to ask him questions.

"How do you train them?"

"With kindness and a large whip."

"Where are they?"

"Here they are, on my lapel. That's King, this is Therbold, and here's Nedleman, my star performer. Watch this. Do a half gainer . . . Do a cartwheel . . . Turn left . . . turn right. Do a handstand."

Just then a woman pushed her way through the crowd and declared, "Performing fleas indeed! You're a fraud!"

Suddenly a flea went *bonk* and flipped right into her hair.

"Help!" the woman screamed.

"Just a moment, madame. Don't panic. That's Nedleman, my star performer. I'll get him out . . . There, Nedleman, that's a good boy. It was a narrow escape."

The woman demanded, "If that's your trained flea, make him do some tricks.

The flea trainer said, "Do a cartwheel, Nedleman."

The flea didn't move.

"Do a handstand."

Nothing.

"Do two or three pushups."

Still nothing.

"Just as I thought," the woman shouted, "a fraud."

"Just a moment, madame. There's been a mistake here. This is not my flea."

The tap dancer was on the same bill with an act that he admired greatly—the Lone Ranger and his horse, Silver. The tap dancer got to the theater early. The Lone Ranger was nowhere in sight, but Silver was standing patiently in the wings. The dancer looked admiringly at the beautiful animal and said out loud, "My, what a beautiful horse!" To his surprise, the horse said, "You think so?" The dancer assured him he did and said, "It must be a real kick to work for the Lone Ranger." The horse snorted and answered, "Big deal! I do all the work and the Lone Ranger gets all the credit. You are looking at a horse that works like a dog." "I had no idea he was such a slave driver." Just then a door could be heard closing and footsteps were heard coming closer. "Shhh," said the horse, "here he comes now, and if he finds out I can talk, he'll have me yelling, 'Hi yo, Silver.'"

An English scientist captured a pink gorilla. He brought it to America and all the members of the press came to see it. "The unusual thing about this gorilla, gentlemen," said the scientist, "is that he also talks the Queen's English. You can go in and have a conference with him but, whatever you do, do not touch the beast." The reporters agreed and went in and started asking him questions. But the man from *The News* just could not resist. When nobody was looking, he walked over and touched the gorilla. The gorilla went insane. He chased the reporter out through a door. The reporter ran frantically down the alley until he came to a brick wall, with no escape possible. The gorilla raised his huge paw and said, "Tag, you're it."

A lobster fell madly in love with a lady crab. Every day he used to go down to her pool with a bouquet of seaweed. He finally professed his love to her and it was arranged that he would meet her father. That evening he knocked on the top of the water and was greeted by a throaty, "Yes, what is it?" "I've come to tell you that I'm dotty about your daughter," replied the lobster. "Well, boy," responded the father crab, "I've got to tell you that it will not work. The lobsters of the world crawl in a nice straight line but crabs always crawl sideways. Biologically the marriage will not work. If there were offspring—God forbid." The disillusioned lobster left the crab pool and was walking depressedly across the sand when suddenly over a little sand dune came his lady crab love. And she walked like a little dream, in a marvelous straight line. "My love," cried the lobster, "we'll be married; you can walk in a straight line." She said with a definite drunken slur to her words, "Whaterya talkin' about walkin' in a straight line?"

A theatrical agent walked into his office and asked his secretary, "Anybody waiting?" She said, "There's a guy outside who has a new act." "Send him in." "Have I got an act for you! Clara the Singing Chicken." "It just looks like a regular chicken," the agent said. The chicken then sang "I'm a Yankee Doodle Dandy . . ." "Does she do anything else?" "Card tricks." The chicken worked for an hour and twenty-five minutes. Its owner finally asked, "Well, what do you think?" "I don't know. Let me see her legs."

The deer and his antelope friend were chasing around on the prairie and having a wonderful time. Suddenly the antelope stopped so short, the deer nearly ran into him, "Hey, what's the matter?" "Shh," said the antelope, "I think I heard a discouraging word."

This momma sardine was showing her baby sardines around the ocean for the first time, so the baby sardines wouldn't be afraid of all the other fish life around. They swam around and the first thing they saw was a shark, and the little sardines didn't get scared. And the next thing was a starfish, and the babies didn't get scared. Even an octopus didn't scare the baby sardines. All of a sudden a submarine went by and the little sardines were scared to death. The mother reassured them, "Don't be afraid, sweethearts, that's a submarine—we call them cans of people."

A man accepted an invitation to be a seventh for poker. When he got to his friend's home, there were only five others there. "I thought you said I'd make a seventh. I'd hate to play a six-handed game." "Don't worry, the sixth player is over there. His name is Jeff." Jeff was a huge labrador retriever. "The dog is going to play poker?" The dog picked up the cards in his paws and shuffled them, cut them and dealt. The man looked at Jeff and said, "Wow, that's a pretty smart dog, isn't it?" "Aw, he ain't so smart; every time he gets a good hand, he wags his tail."

2
He's So Dumb That . . .

There was an old lay from Wheeling
Who had a peculiar feeling
That she was a fly
And wanted to try
To walk upside down on the ceiling.

Two friends who lived together stared out of the window after a great snow storm.

One said, "My goodness, somebody filled our driveway with snow. We can't take the car out today."

And his friend said, "I think we can shovel it all away."

They got two shovels and started to work, and kept at it for about four hours. Finally one said, "There's got to be a better way. Why don't we get a bucket and go to the gas station and get some gasoline. Then we can burn all the snow away."

His friend agreed. "That's a good idea."

They got a bucket from the garage and started pushing their way through the snow. After about ten minutes one of them stopped and shook his head. "Hold it," he said. "It's no good. It won't work."

"Why won't it work?"

"If we burn it, we'll have to shovel away the ashes."

The challenger was taking a real beating and by the fifth round he was losing badly. Then a right to the jaw dropped him flat on his back. The referee came over and started

21

counting: "One . . . two . . . three . . ." The challenger turned over and raised himself to one knee, shook his head and tried to get up. From the corner his manager yelled at him, "Stay down until eight! Don't get up until eight!" The challenger looked up, nodded, and said, "O.K. What time is it now?"

A panhandler, instead of asking for the usual dime for the usual cup of coffee, asked, "Will you give me fifteen cents for a sandwich." The man answered, "I don't know; let me see the sandwich."

The antique collector had just bought a priceless grandfather's clock. He couldn't wait to have it delivered; he was so anxious to get it home. But it was too tall and too bulky to fit even into a Checker cab, so he had to carry it home on his back. Suddenly a drunk lurched into him. The grandfather's clock crashed to the pavement and broke into little pieces.

The man was furious, "Why don't you look where you are going?"

The drunk just peered at him and said, "Why don't you wear a wristwatch like everybody else?"

Two fellows met and one of them said, "I've been looking at your car. It's the craziest paint job I ever saw. You've got the right side painted green and the left side painted yellow. What's the idea?" The other said, "I know it doesn't look good but, in case of an accident, you should hear the witnesses contradict each other."

The college team had a fifth-string quarterback whom they used for practicing. Every day at practice this fellow really took a beating. One day the coach said, "Look, Mellman, you've been coming out every day for four years, and practicing with the team here. We all know good football and good sportsmanship go hand in hand, so we'll let you play in the game tomorrow." "Oh, boy! I'm ready! I'm ready." The coach said, "Tell me, Mellman, what will you do if we have the ball and there is time for only one more play, the score is nothing to nothing, and it's the fourth down?" And Mellman said, "Well, I'd slide down to the end of the bench so I could see better."

Bartenders are the world's friendliest and most tactful people. They are usually pretty good at taking people as they come, and they see all kinds of strange things. Like a bartender I know. He was busy cleaning up one day when he looked up and there, standing at the bar, was a man with a potato sticking out of each ear. The bartender thought to himself: "He wants me to ask him what he's doing with the potatoes in his ears. I'm not going to fall for it." The man had a beer and went out. The next night the man came in again, this time with two potatoes in each ear. The bartender didn't say a word. For five nights the man came in with potatoes in his ears, drank a beer, then went out. On the sixth night he came in with two pieces of celery sticking out of his ears. The bartender flipped.

"All right," he says, "you come in here five nights with potatoes. Now how come you have celery in your ears?"

The man shrugged. "The doctor told me to stay away from fattening foods."

An old farmer who came to New York for the first time had never been inside a big hotel. He wandered about the lobby for a while and then stopped before a row of elevators. He really didn't know what they were. But as he stood there puzzling over the doors that kept sliding open and shut, a darling, little old lady of about 84 hobbled by him and got into the elevator. He watched the doors close behind her. After a while the doors opened and a beautiful blonde stepped out.

"Drat!" he said. "I wish I'd brought my old lady along."

A husband was taking his wife to her first ball game, the deciding game of the World Series, no less. She was late getting dressed. The subway was jammed and just poked along. By the time they reached the ball park, the game was almost over. He fought his way to his seat, his wife trailing behind him. "What's going on?" he asked the man in the seat next to theirs. "It's the last of the ninth, the score is zero-zero, and both pitchers are pitching no-hitters." "Wonderful," said the wife. "We haven't missed anything."

An Englishman driving across America pulled into a gas station. An old-timer leaning up against the side of the pump was waving a little kerchief back and forth.

"Hello."

"Howdy."

"Beautiful country around here. I couldn't help noticing that kerchief you have there. What do you use it for?"

"A weather gauge."

"How can you possibly tell the weather with a kerchief dangling from your hand?"

"Simple. If the kerchief moves back and forth, it's windy. If it gets wet, it's usually raining."

Two Hollywood producers were having a very serious discussion about the casting of their latest picture. They were having a particularly difficult time deciding who would play the male lead. An oddball little man had been standing around, just listening. All of a sudden he said, "Hey, why don't you fellows use John Barrymore?" They looked down at him and said, "John Barrymore is dead." "Oh, is he still dead?"

Clyde and his friend were talking, and Clyde said, "Golly, I really need some new shoes for the dance Saturday night." Clyde's friend said, "So, why don't we go down to the shoestore and get some alligator shoes." "OK." They went in, and Clyde asked, "How much are the alligator shoes in the window?" The clerk said, "Only $100." "Gosh! I only have $25. Well, never mind." The friends walked out and Clyde's pal said, "Hey, you know, where we live we've got a lot of alligators. Why don't we catch one?" Clyde said, "Swell idea!" They walked to the friend's house and sat down by the swamp. Suddenly Clyde saw an alligator just slipping along. He jumped right on its back, shouting, "I got you!" And he held on and he fought and he finally pulled the alligator out on the bank. Then he kicked it right back into the swamp. His friend demanded, "What'd you do that for?" "Well, wouldn't you know, with my luck, I had to pick on one that was barefooted."

He was a lovely man whose whole world was music, and who knew nothing about sports, or even seemed to care about sports. His son walked into the house one night and found him watching a basketball game on TV. Astonished, the son asked his father, "What are you looking at?" "A basketball game." "What's the score?" "One hundred and two to ninety eight." "Who's winning?" "One hundred and two."

This fellow walked out of the golf pro shop and said to a friend, "I just got a set of clubs for my wife." "Hey, you made a heck of a good trade."

A salesman in a hurry hired a small, private airplane to fly him home. Sitting beside the pilot, he tried to make conversation.

"You seem to know your job. Have you been flying long?"

"Oh, about three months."

"That's interesting. New pilot, eh? What did you do before you took up flying?"

"I was in an institution."

The passenger turned white. "An . . . an institution?"

"Yeh. But don't worry. I'm all right now."

"Glad to hear that," the passenger said, not really convinced. "What's that on your left wrist?"

"A compass to keep me from getting lost."

"I see. And that thing you have on your right wrist?"

"That's a mirror."

"A mirror?"

"Sure. I look in it and that's how I know who's lost."

The two drunks reeled out of the bar and staggered

down the street. They wove their way from the gutter to the building walls and out again. Just as they approached the corner of the block, one drunk stumbled down the subway stairs. His friend didn't notice his disappearance until he had managed to cross the street against the light. He looked around for his friend. Just as he was about to stagger on, he saw his friend crawling up the subway stairs. "Hey, you, where you been?" "Me? I jusht walked through some guy's basement, and boy, that guy's sure got some set a trains."

Two brothers bought themselves horses but they couldn't tell them apart. One brother said, "I know a good way to mark which is which. I'm gonna hit my horse in the eye." So he gave his horse a black eye. The next day the other brother's horse fell and gave himself a black eye. Again they had the same problem. Now one brother suggested, "I'll take an axe and cut off my horse's tail." He did, and they were able to tell the horses apart, but not for long. The following day the other horse backed into a thresher and lost his tail. The first brother said, "This is ridiculous! I'll knock my horse's teeth out and that'll do it." So he did, but the other horse got some kind of disease and lost his teeth.

Well, to this day those two brothers don't know which horse is whose, the white one or the brown one.

A man went into a department store and walked over to one of the clerks and said, "Ex-ex-cuse me-me p-p-pl-pl-please, I want t-t-to b-b-buy two suits." The clerk said, "Third floor in back, you can't miss it. I don't want to seem personal or anything, but I notice that you have a little speech impediment." "How-how-how could you tell? It's b-b-been twenty-two years and no d-d-doctor has b-b-been able to help me." The clerk said, "There is a wonderful speech school in this city. Why don't you go to it? Maybe they'll be able to help you." "G-g-gee, that w-w-would b-b-be wonderful. Wh-where is it?" The clerk told him and the man left. Six months later he came back to the same store, went up to the same salesman, and said, "Hey, mister, Peter Piper picked a peck of pickled peppers." The clerk said, "Gee, that's marvelous. They certainly helped your speech." "Yeah, b-b-but w-w-w-what g-g-good does it do to g-g-go around s-s-saying that all d-d-day long."

The policeman picked up a suspicious character. "I'm going to take you down to the station unless you explain what you're up to." "I didn't do anything, officer." "Oh, yeh? I saw you go into that store with a hundred dollar bill and get them to change it to two fifties." "That's right." "Then you went into the store next door and had them change the two fifties back into a hundred dollar bill." "Sure. But is that against the law?" "Then you went into another store and had the hundred changed into ten tens. Another store changed it back to a hundred dollar bill. And you went into a store farther down the street and got five twenties." "That's right." "Well, what's the idea? What are you up to?" "That's easy, officer. One of these days somebody is going to make a mistake . . . and it isn't going to be me."

A kook drove up the curb, parked his car, got out, locked all the doors, and then realized that he had left the keys inside. "Oh, rats! Let me think. How am I going to get into my car? I'll have to break a window, that's what I'll do. But first I better call the garage." He called his garage and told the mechanic that he had locked his keys inside the car. "I'm wondering which window I should break to get in."

"Don't break any window. We have skeleton keys for every car."

"I'd be much obliged if you came and opened the door for me."

"Stay where you are and we'll be down to unlock the car for you."

"All right. But please, please hurry. You see, it's starting to rain and I left the top down."

A man spent the evening out with the fellows and he was feeling good, but he thought to himself, "I'm getting home pretty late to start with and if my wife sees me in this condition, I'm in a world of trouble." At the bus stop was a coffee vending machine. He dropped a dime in and pushed the button for coffee, with cream and extra sugar. Little lights flashed on the machine, and the mechanism started to hum. Out came first coffee, then the cream, and next a little hand came out and dropped two cubes of sugar. But there was no cup. He shook his head and said, "How do you like that? Automation is really wonderful. The darn thing drinks it for you."

The church bells kept ringing and ringing. People in the street were going crazy. Finally one man climbed up into the steeple, and there was this man ringing and ringing the bells. "Why are you ringing the bells? Is this some kind of holiday?"

"No."

"Well, is somebody getting married?"

"No."

"Then why are the bells ringing?"

"Because I'm pulling the rope."

The two drunks had been assigned a room on the fifth-floor of the hotel. The bar was on the street floor, naturally, but they decided they just had to have another nightcap. They staggered down the corridor to the elevator. Somehow, though the elevator car was on the seventh floor, the fifth-floor door had been left open. One drunk stepped through the open door, and fell to the bottom of the shaft. His friend peered down at him and said, "Are you sure that's the right way to get down to the bar?" "Sure it is. But be careful on that first step. It's a beaut."

A man walked into a lumber yard and said, "I want to buy some boards." The lumber salesman asked, "How many you want?" "I don't know." "Well, you'll have to figure it out." "I will." So the man left. He came back after a while and said, "I want 85 of them." "What kind of wood?" "I don't know." "Well, you'd better make up your mind." "I will." The man went away. After a while he came back and said, "I want maple." "Fine, but how long do you want them?" "I don't know, but I'll find out." When he came back, he said, "I want them a long time; we're going to build a house."

A man standing on a corner had a banana sticking in each ear. Everyone kept looking at him. Finally one person couldn't hold his curiosity, "Excuse me, buddy, but why do you have a banana sticking in each ear?" "What?" "Why do you have a banana sticking in each ear?" "I'm sorry, I couldn't understand you. What?" "Why do you have a banana in each ear?" "Would you please speak up. I can't hear too well; you see I have a banana in each ear."

A man walked down the street making sounds like a clock. Another man stopped him and wanted to know, "What's the matter with you?" "I'm a clock." "A clock?" "Yes." "Well, what time is it?" "It's exactly one twenty-two." "That's wrong, it's one twenty-five." "Oh? I must be slow."

Count Basie's band was at the Dallas airport, waiting for their flight out after a one-night stand. To while away the time, one of the musicians wandered over to a fortune-telling weighing machine. He put in his money, weighed himself, but instead of getting a little card with his fortune on it he heard a voice saying: "You are a black American, a musician. You are 47 years old and you weigh 150 pounds. You are on your way by air to Chicago." The musician was impressed but not convinced the answer had not been a fluke. So he walked over to an American Indian who was also waiting and persuaded him to weigh himself on the same machine. The voice said: "You are a red-blooded American Indian of Mohawk descent. You make fine carpets and you are on your way to Phoenix." The Indian remained impassive, but the musician was excited, "I'm going to fool that machine! Quick—lend me your blanket and your headdress." The musician put on the headdress, wrapped himself in the blanket, stepped back on the scale, put in his coin and waited for his fortune. This time the voice said: "You are still a black American and a musician. You are still 47 and still weigh 150. While you were playing around with that blanket, you missed your plane to Chicago."

The reporter for the local paper was interviewing the residents of a farming community right at the time of the successful Apollo 11 flight to the moon. He stopped one farmer obviously in town to do the week's shopping, "Hey, there, how about what's going on on the moon?" The farmer looked at him a moment, then said, "Did the cow jump over it again?"

Two truck drivers pulled into a place where truck drivers often stop for coffee. They sat at the counter bragging about how fast and how big their trucks were. One said, "Yeah, I just came from Lancaster to L.A. and made it in four hours." "Aw, you couldn't do that—you'd have to go over 100 mph." Suddenly, a great big, streamlined truck, screeched into the drive-in. "That's McAllister." "Who's McAllister?" "A guy who works for our trucking unit. He's from Texas, and you think *we* brag about how fast our trucks go. This guy will knock you dead." McAllister came in and never said a word. He sat there and drank his coffee. The others all waited for him to start bragging. They asked, "How long you been driving?" "Three days." "Making good time?" "OK." Not getting much response, they were ready to leave when suddenly a jet roared over the diner and McAllister went insane. "What's the matter with you?" "What's the matter with me? Are you kidding? I've stopped once a day for three days to have coffee and every time I stop, he catches up."

Some of the patients at a rest home were building a wall to make the place look a little better. Eight men each had a barrow, and they'd go over to a big pile, fill up with bricks and tote them to those who were working on the wall. The ninth man had a wheelbarrow too, but his was upside down. He'd get in line, but since there was no place to put the bricks he'd walk over empty. People laughed at him: "Hey, why don't you turn your barrow the right way up like the others?" "What do you think I am, crazy? If I do that, they fill it with bricks."

On his very first visit to Key West, the man tried skin diving. He became an enthusiast: he bought an aqua lung, took lessons, the whole bit. The first time out with a mask, and he dove down about 40 feet. There, swimming around he met a friend of his, also swimming around, but with no skin-diving equipment. He swam over and said, "Golberg, my goodness, what are you doing 40 feet under the water without skin-diving equipment?" "Idiot! What do you think I'm doing? I'm drowning!"

A farmer had the scariest scarecrow anyone had ever seen. His neighbor came over one day and asked, "Why on earth do you have such a frightening scarecrow? The kids are all terrified." "I'll tell you why I've got it. It's to scare the giraffes away." "What are you? An idiot? I've lived here twenty-three years and I haven't seen one giraffe." "You see, it works."

Two men met in the street. One of them was carrying a bag.

The other said, "Tell me something, what have you got in the bag?"

"I won't tell you."

"Well, how about if I guess?"

"Good idea."

"Well, have you got a house in there?"

"No."

"Do you have a horse?"

"No."

"I give up. Tell me—what's in the bag?"

He said, "I have chickens in the bag."

"Can I have one?"

"No."

"Well, if I guess how many chickens are in the bag, can I have one?"

The man with the bag said, "If you guess how many chickens are in the bag, I'll give you both of them."

The other said, "Five?"

Two friends applied for a job as a truck-driving team. "I'm Sam and this is Nero. When I drive at night, he sleeps." The prospective employer said, "All right, I'll give you a chance. But, first, I'll give you an oral test. Suppose you're driving along at three o'clock in the morning, and you're on a little bridge when, all of a sudden, a big trailer truck comes at you at 100 miles an hour. What is the first thing you'd do?" Sam said, "I'd wake up my partner, Nero." "Why?" "He never saw a wreck like that before."

The man had been knocked down by a hit-and-run driver. A passer-by walked over and looked at him lying in the gutter. "Have an accident?" "No thanks, I just had one."

At the beginning of the space race there was a lot of preoccupation with rockets. A country bumpkin came to New York City, and when he saw the Empire State Building with its revolving doors, said: "I don't care how fast they spin those little propellers, they'll never get that thing off the ground."

The high school football star had flunked all his exams and so the principal had to rule him ineligible for the big game. The coach was upset. He took the big kid by the hand and led him to the principal's office. "Sir, if you don't let this boy play, we'll lose the ninth time in a row. Give the boy a chance."

The principal said, "I've got as much pride in our school team as anybody. I'll ask him a simple question. If he answers it right, I'll let him play." He turned to the boys and said, "All right, son. Tell me, how much is two plus two?"

The boy thought a moment and said, "Six!"

"Sorry," said the principal. "I can't let him play."

The coach pleaded, "Aw, come on, give him a break. He's only one off."

The dowager was waiting for an elevator and it didn't come fast enough to please her. Finally, when the doors opened, she stepped in and asked arrogantly, "Young man, where have you been?" "Lady, where can you go in an elevator?"

Joe and Bill met on a street corner. When Joe said he sure was glad to see his friend, Bill answered:

"How can you see me when I'm not even here? And I'll bet you $10 dollars I can prove it!"

"You're going to bet me $10 that you're not here? Okay, it's a bet. Go ahead and prove it."

"Am I in Chicago?"

"Nope."

"Am I in New York?"

Joe answered emphatically, "No!"

"Well, if I'm not in Chicago and I'm not in New York, that means I'm in some other place, right?"

"That's right."

"Well, if I'm in some other place, I can't be here. I'll take that $10."

"How can I give you the money if you're not here."

Two counterfeiters were printing busily. Suddenly one of them looked closely at one of the bills and exclaimed, "You idiot! These are *sixteen*-dollar bills." The other man was dumbfounded, but after a moment's thought came up with an idea. "Why don't we take them to a small village up in the mountains. Those people are so dumb they'll take a sixteen-dollar bill." So they drove up into the mountains in Vermont. They stopped before a General Store and walked in, and one of the counterfeiters said to the old man behind the counter, "I wonder if you can help us. We're from the city. I've just lost a bet to my friend and I have to pay him but all I've got is a sixteen-dollar bill. I wonder if you could break it for me?" "I'd be glad to. How would you like it, two eights or four fours?"

The bereaved lady had recently lost her husband. Going

through his belongings, she found a picture that had been taken of him when he was about 24 or 25. She said, "It's the only picture I've got of Willis." Her friend said, "Why don't you take that picture to a photographer? He'll retouch it, enlarge it. It will be as though Willis is in the room." The widow said, "That's wonderful." So she went to the photographer and said, "Do you do all those marvelous things with photographs?" He said, "We certainly do." She said, "This picture is of my Willis. Of course, when he passed away he didn't have the moustache, the hat or the vest, but my friend said you could remove all that." "We certainly can." "Well, take out the moustache, paint out the bowtie, and maybe remove the hat." "All right. Would you tell me, please, what side your husband parted his hair?" "Young man, don't you know your business? You'll see that when you take his hat off."

A man reading a paper says, "Hey, man, there's a doctor in Houston, Texas, who considers the brain to be the most important part of the body. I don't think it's the most important part of a body, do you?" And his friend answers, "No, I never considered the brain the most important part of the body. The most important part to me is the mouth. If you don't have a mouth and you're drinking soup, it goes all over your shirt." The man who had been reading says, "It's not the most important part to me. The most important part of my body to me is the dimples in my knees." "What makes them so important?" "I eat celery in bed and that's where I keep the salt."

A lot of people don't know that Australia is larger than the United States. And yet there are fewer than 12 million people in the whole country. So naturally ranches there are big—one is larger than the State of Texas. Australians are particularly proud of their sheep ranches. One visitor was being shown all the marvels of one of these ranches—stations, they call them down there. He was impressed, "Look at those thousands of sheep! You must know everything there is to be known about sheep." "Yes, we certainly do. Do you know it takes three sheep just to make one sweater?" "That's really remarkable. And I didn't even know they could knit."

It was late at night and the Englishman was sound asleep in his home when suddenly there was a knock at the door. He opened the door and the man standing there said, "Hi, how are you?" "I'm fine, but what the devil are you doing knocking on my door at three o'clock in the morning?" "Aren't you Sir Harris Manning?" "Yes, I am." "Didn't you put an ad in the paper advertising for a partner to go hunting with you?" "Yes, I did." "And you're going to go to Africa and hunt lions and tigers and elephants and boa constrictors and everything?" "Yes, what of it?" "I just want to tell you that under no circumstance will I go with you."

A married couple went for a vacation way down South. They checked into a hotel and decided to call some friends back home. The local operator would get on the phone and say, "Yes, is there any number I can get for you-all?" And they'd tell her the number and invariably the one they reached was a wrong number. They asked for fifteen numbers and fifteen times they got a wrong one. Finally they gave up and went to sleep. In the middle of the night, the phone rang. The fellow picked it up and said, "Hello, what? Yeah. No thanks." He hung up. His wife asked, "Who was that." "Same operator; said she had some right numbers and wanted to know if we could use them."

A Texan threw something over his shoulder as he walked away from the Trevi Fountain in Rome. His wife asked, "How big a coin did you throw, honey?" "Who threw a coin? I wrote a check."

Moe Noodleman was a baseball buff. He was the kind who, when a pitcher threw a ball, would turn to anyone who would listen and explain that that was the 717th slider that pitcher had thrown in the past three years and 413 of them had been on Tuesdays. One day friends convinced Moe that he should go out to the racetrack, watch the horses and maybe even bet. He went out and, as novices usually do, picked a long shot—a 50-to-1 long shot. Sure enough, when the horses got to the sixteenth pole on the way in, it had become a very close race. The 50-to-1 shot and the favorite were running neck and neck. They were nose to nose almost at the finish line when Moe Noodleman jumped up and yelled: "Slide, you bum, slide!"

This horse addict was always winning the long odds, and his bookie was going crazy and losing money. The bookie wanted to find out what the system was, so he asked the man one day, "Listen, you're always winning a lot of money on the horses. How do you do it?" "Well, I take a scratch sheet of the horses that are going to race and I put it up on the wall. Then I take a handkerchief and I blindfold myself, then I take a pin and stab the sheet. Whatever name the pin lands, that's the horse I bet on." "Yeah, but yesterday you had four winners in a row. How did you do that?" "Same system, but instead of a pin I used a fork."

This is the story of the man who was driving down a country road, bothering no one, when he suddenly heard cries for help. He pulled over to the side and got out of his car to see who was in trouble. A man was sitting in a tree near the edge of the road, holding on to the limbs desperately and calling for help at the top of his voice. And standing at the base of the tree was another man.

"Hey! What's going on here?"

The man in the tree said: "Listen. That fellow standing under me is crazy. He thinks he's driving a car."

"That's his problem. Why don't you come down?"

"Oh, yeh? And have him run me over?"

3

Now Hear This . . .

A Republican out on his motor
Ran over a Democrat voter.
"Thank goodness," he cried,
"He was on the wrong side,
So I don't blame myself one ioter."

The fellow had never wanted to be in the Army. Even when he saluted, he gave himself a headache. Finally, they got him to the front lines, but when he saw the guns going off and the tanks and the airplanes, he decided, "This is no place for me." He started running back from the front. He ran and ran until suddenly somebody grabbed his arm. "Wait a minute, son, where do you think you're going?" The soldier said, "I'm getting as far back as I can." The man who had stopped him said, "Do you know who I am?" "No." "I'm the general." The soldier said, "I didn't know I was that far back."

The soldier had been thrown into the brig. A friend who came to see him asked, "What's the matter? How come you're in here?" "I don't know. It's been terrible. I hate it." "Well, how did you get in here?" "For obeying an order. My sergeant said, 'If it moves, salute it, if it doesn't move, lift it, and if it's too big to lift, paint it'." "Well, what's wrong with that?" "I painted the general's wife."

During the Israeli Six Day War, five Arabs pounced on an

37

Israeli soldier, who proceeded to beat the devil out of them. As the Arabs ran away, the Israeli soldier shouted after them, "Lucky my husband didn't catch you."

Two Russians were having a philosophical discussion. One said to the other, "Tell me something, comrade. I promise not to report it even to my wife. Have you read the Bible?"

"If this is just between you and me, my friend, the answer is yes. . . ." He glanced over his shoulder carefully and added, "I pride myself, as a scholar, that I know something about the Bible."

"Good. Perhaps you can tell what nationality were Adam and Eve?"

"Without a doubt, my friend, they were Russians."

"You're sure?"

"Absolutely!"

"What makes you so sure?"

"The evidence. They didn't have anything to wear, all they had to eat was an apple—and they thought they were living in Paradise."

An astronaut was being interviewed after coming back from outer space. "How was the trip?" he was asked. "How did you feel up there?"

"Well, how would you feel hundreds of thousands of miles away from earth if you were in a space capsule made up of hundreds of tiny electronic parts and computers and transisters—all made by the lowest bidder?"

During the war a pilot in a disabled plane was coming in to land: "Pilot to tower, pilot to tower." "Tower to pilot, what's the matter?" "Lost half of left wing, whole screen and canopy gone, and losing fuel. Request instructions." "Better prepare for forced landing. Reduce speed and approach field." "Pilot to tower! Emergency, all engines have stopped, tail section fallen away. What instructions?" "Repeat after me, 'Dearly beloved. . . .'"

A man walked up to a farmer as he came out of a voting

booth, "I'm from the FBI." "What seems to be the trouble?" "We happen to know that you accepted a bribe and sold your vote." "That's not true. I voted for the candidate because I like him." "Well, that's where we've got you. We have concrete evidence that you accepted fifty dollars from him." "Well, it's plain common sense, if someone gives you fifty dollars, you're going to like him."

A couple of policeman cruising in a patrol car had not given out a ticket all day long. Finally one said, "Next car that comes by, we're going to give the driver a ticket. We don't care what happens." A car came by and they followed it, but the driver did everything correctly—stopped at the light and gave hand signals before he turned. The cops were amazed: "Can't believe it. This is the greatest thing in the world. This must be the mayor." They pulled him over and said, "Pardon us, sir, we don't want to give you a ticket. You were driving amazingly well. One of the finest drivers we have seen in the state. We want to commend you and thank you for obeying all of the laws." The driver replied, "When you're as loaded as I am you have to drive carefully."

The rookie came back to camp after a day's leave. He stood there, lined up for review. The colonel spotted him, and he looked at him and said, "Hey, you, Noodleman, look at you, look at your torn uniform, look at your blood-shot eyes, look at your dirty shoes, who ever told you that you're a soldier?" And Noodleman looked up at him and said, "My draft board."

He had done everything he could to evade the draft, but he finally had to go for his physical. So he went down and he played nutty, he couldn't hear, he limped, he did everything wrong. Nothing worked. Finally he got to the eye doctor. And the eye doctor said, "All right, son, look at that chart up there on that wall." "What chart? And what wall?" The doctor said, "Fine, you're in the Army, boy." "But, Doc, wait a minute, I can't see. "The doctor replied, "That's all right, son; we'll put you all the way up front so you can see the whole thing."

A tough sergeant who had just gotten out of the Army was hired to supervise riflery practice at a military school for boys. The day he arrived there, he lined up all the cadets: "All right now, I'm your sergeant. I'm going to teach you how to use those rifles. From now on good marksmanship and good cadets go hand in hand. Now get down on your knees with the rifle and you'll shoot at the target from 250 yards." So all the boys got down, they all shot, and they all missed the target. "OK. Everybody, 100 yards up closer." They all moved up. And they shot. They all missed the target again. "OK. Attention. Fix bayonets and charge. It's your only chance."

The President had managed to elude the Secret Service men to do a little quiet fishing. Suddenly a thunderstorm came up. High winds churned the water, and the President's rowboat was swamped. He did not know how to swim. All his desperate flailing was barely keeping him afloat. In the nick of time three young fellows in an outboard rescued him. The President was grateful: "I am very grateful for all that you fellows did, and I want to show my appreciation. Anything you want I'll see you get." "I'd like an appointment to West Point," said one of the three. "It's yours," said the President. The second young man just didn't want to go to war and he didn't want to evade the draft. "Don't worry, you won't be called," the President assured him. Turning to the third young man, he asked, "And what do you want?" "A military funeral." "A military funeral?" "Yes. When my old man finds out what I have done, he's going to kill me."

The court-martial was being held to try a lieutenant and a private, both being charged with the same offense—hitting their commanding officer right on the jaw. The colonel sitting as judge said to the lieutenant, "Tell me in your own words what happened." "Sir, I have this excruciatingly painful corn on my right foot. The captain was walking by and he stepped right on that corn. I saw red. I couldn't control myself, so I hit him right on the jaw." The judge turned to the private, "And what was your reason for hitting the captain?" "Well, sir, I saw the lieutenant here hit him, so I hit him too. I thought the war was over, sir."

The soldier walked along as if he were looking for something: "Nope, that's not it. Nope, that's not it. Nope, that's not it."

An officer saw him and asked, "What's that clown doing out there?" Another soldier answered, "We don't know, sir. But he's been that way ever since he was transferred here. For weeks he does nothing but go around picking up things, shaking his head and saying, "Nope, that's not it.'" "Well," said the officer, "Get him to a doctor."

The soldier was taken to the doctor who placed him under observation. For three weeks he was kept in the hospital. All that time he walked around, poking into everything, looking everywhere, and saying, "Nope, that's not it. Nope, that's not it." Finally the doctor called him into his office. "Son, we've been watching you. Now, please don't get upset about what I have to tell you. We can find nothing physically wrong with you. It's just that you do not fit into the Armed Forces. So we're going to give you your discharge. Sign this form and take it over to headquarters."

The soldier took the sheet and looked at it and said, "That's it. That's it."

The President ordered his special helicopter to take him over to the airfield to his private plane. As he boarded Air Force I, the pilot came to him for his orders. "Good morning, Mr. President, where are we going?" The Preisdent replied, "Oh, take me anywhere. We've got troubles all over."

Three nuclear physicists decided they needed a vacation. They drove from Alamogordo to Las Vegas. Two of the three decided they would rather spend the evening at one of the famous nightclubs and see the floor show. The third said he would go and do a little gambling at one of the casinos. Having wined and dined and seen the floor show twice, the two friends returned to their hotel. The third man had not yet come in so they went out looking for him. At the tenth casino they went into, they saw their friend at the roulette wheel. They walked over to watch him play. He had obviously been winning a lot, and he was still winning. The croupier called the two over to him and said, "Will you please take your friend out of here—he's playing like there will be no tomorrow." The two physicists looked at each other and one said, "I wonder if he knows something we don't."

A very fragile young man who should never have been allowed to leave home got into basic training under a lieutenant who was a real man-eater. He used to go around yelling and growling. The rookies were all having their guns inspected, and the lieutenant was yelling as usual, walking along and putting everyone on report. He suddenly came to a halt in front of the fragile young man and said, "Give me that gun, soldier." And then he slammed it right back at him. "Take a look. Take a look at that gun." The fellow looked at it and held it up, and finally said, "Oh, my goodness, it's got a hole right through it."

In a small country in the Middle East, the party in power happened to have a man at its head who was a great optimist. The country was really bankrupt and things were going from bad to worse. But at a meeting of the cabinet the leader got up and proposed a plan to solve all their problems.

"Gentlemen, I have a great idea and it will solve all our financial difficulties." The members of the cabinet held their breath as he continued. "Tomorrow, at exactly nine o'clock in the morning, we shall declare war on the United States."

"Declare war on the strongest nation in the world?" The cabinet members were aghast. "We don't have a chance!"

"Exactly," the leader declared. "We shall lose, naturally. And what does the United States do with every country it defeats? It lends them money, builds roads, finances all sorts of business projects, sets up schools, hospitals, housing projects. In a few years we shall be as prosperous as Japan, or Germany . . ."

All but one of the ministers applauded enthusiastically. The lone dissenter shook his head and said, "What if we should win?"

At a party, this total bore was monopolizing the entire conversation. Anyone would have thought that he had won the war single-handed. He told one anecdote after another of how he had done this, that and the other thing. He was a big hero. At last one old lady present had had it. As he was going strong on another story—"I was shot down in the Pacific and lived for a whole week on a can of sardines"— she asked, "Weren't you afraid of falling off?"

A Navy lieutenant lost his gun out on the firing range. The captain called him over and said, "You are going to have to pay for that; it's government equipment." "What do you mean, I'm going to have to pay for it? I can't help it if I lost it." "You're going to have to pay for it." "What would happen if I were out riding in a jeep and I went in to get a cup of coffee, and I came out to find that somebody had stolen the jeep. Would I have to pay for that too?" "Yup, you have to pay for any equipment, anything you got that you lose, you have to pay for it." "No wonder the captain always goes down with the ship."

A sergeant was drilling a bunch of rookies; and they were the worst: they dropped their guns, they bumped into each other. Finally in desperation the drill sergeant looked at them and said, "At ease." But they didn't know what he meant. "Just take it easy. I want to tell you a story. When I was a little kid, I had a bunch of little lead soldiers, all broken miserable little lead soldiers. But I loved them. One day the kid next door to me got sick, and I loaned him my little lead soldiers, these miserable lead soldiers to play with. And he fell in love with them and he wouldn't give them back. And I cried; I wanted my little lead soldiers back. And my mother told me not to worry; someday I'd have those little broken miserable soldiers back. . . . And, gentlemen, today you are here."

A very new soldier was on sentry duty at the main gate of a military outpost. His orders were clear: no car was to enter unless it had a special sticker on the windshield. A great big Army car came up with a general seated in the back. The sentry said, "Halt, who goes there?" So the chauffeur, a corporal, said, "General Wheeler." "I'm sorry, I can't let you through. You've got to have a sticker on the windshield." The general said, "Drive on." The sentry said, "Hold it. You really can't come through. I have orders to shoot if you try driving in without a sticker." The general repeated, "I'm telling you, son, drive on." The sentry walked up to the rear window, and said, "General, I'm new at this. Whom do I shoot, you or the driver?"

The chairman introduced the speaker: "Ladies and gentlemen, I now would like to introduce Senator Howard B. Swindlebacker." The Senator came to the podium. "Mr. Chairman, honored guests, I am against taxes, and I have a five-year prison record to back up everything." A voice from the rear interrupted: "Just a minute, Senator, what are you doing about the war on poverty?" "I'm glad you asked. Just yesterday, we captured over 500 beggars."

The man heard a fierce pounding on his door in the middle of the afternoon. He opened the door and a friend of his ran in stark naked, and bruised all over. "What happened?" "I was watching an election parade and all of a sudden two men grabbed me from behind and started beating me. They took my watch and my shoes and all my clothes." "Why didn't you yell?" "Yell? And have those politicians think I was cheering them?"

The infantry was in North Africa. A volunteer was needed to go into the desert to try and capture the Desert Fox, Rommel. No one was anxious to go into the desert. Finally a buck private stepped up and said, "I'll go. I'm your boy. I'll bring that Rommel back. Give me some provisions, and I'll go."

"All right, Max," the lieutenant said. "You've got the job."

They loaded food, water and a wireless on a camel and cheered Max as he set out on his mission. Two days later headquarters received a message from Max: "Rommel captured . . . Rommel captured."

The camp went wild with joy. That would shorten the war and maybe they'd be getting home soon.

Three days passed, then a week. No Max. Another week, two, three weeks. No Max. And then they saw a dot on the horizon. Gradually it got bigger and bigger and they recognized Max, on foot.

"Max! Max! Where's Rommel? Where's Rommel?"

"What Rommel?" Max said. "I've been walking for weeks . . ."

"But we got a message from you—'Rommel captured . . . Rommel captured.' "

"You're crazy. The message was 'Camel ruptured . . . camel ruptured.' "

A Congressman was awakened in the middle of the night by his wife: "I think there's a burglar in the house." "My dear," he said, "There are no burglars in the House; in the Senate, yes."

The recruit had been assigned to a garage job at one of the army camps. When the phone rang, he answered: "Hello." The voice on the other end said, "What have you got down there in the garage?" "Well, let me see now. . . We've got some jeeps, and we've got us some semis, and we've got us some of those big Cadillacs that those dumb-dumb generals ride around in." The voice on the other end asked,

"Do you know who you're talking to?" And the boy said, "No, sir, I don't." "This happens to be General Bradford." The recruit swallowed and said, "Do you know who you're talking to?" And the general said, "No, of course not." "So long, dumb-dumb."

A couple in Russia had a potato farm and everything was going well until he got into trouble politically and he had to escape to West Berlin. There he received a secret note from his wife: "Dear Boris, we are very hungry. We don't know what to do, because I have no one to help me plant the potatoes. What should I do?" He wrote back, "Don't worry, darling. Everything will be OK. Don't touch the field because, remember, the shortwave radio and all the guns are hidden there." Naturally the secret police read the letter, and immediately dug up the whole field. She wrote her husband what had happened, and he wrote back: "Dear Sonia, Now that the field has been plowed, you can plant potatoes."

A nationally known politician was the principal speaker at a store-front rally. Afterward, he shook hands with people in the crowd, and walked through the neighborhood. He saw a boy sitting on a curb with a box full of squirming puppies beside him. The politician walked over and said, "Hello, son, are those your pups?" "Yes, sir, and I'm trying to sell them." "What kind of pups are they?" "Oh, they're good Republican pups." "Republicans, eh? How much are they?" "Twenty-five cents apiece." "I'll take two for my kids." A few weeks later, the politician was back in the neighborhood. There was the same kid with the remaining puppies. The politician watched as a passer-by stopped and asked, "What kind of pups are they and how much do you want for one?" "They are Democrats and I want seventy-five cents." The man laughed and bought a puppy. The politician walked over to the boy and said, "A few weeks ago, you told me those pups were Republicans and you sold me two for only twenty-five cents apiece." "Yes, sir, but now they have their eyes open."

At a testimonial dinner given for a Chinese statesman in a small Midwestern town, the guest of honor was seated next to a local politician. And the politician wanted to make conversation, so during the meal he leaned over to the Chinese and asked, "You likee soupee?" The statesman just looked at him and smiled. "You likee fruit cupee?" Again the Chinese smiled. A few minutes later the politician asked, "You likee steakee?" The Chinese statesman smiled. The dinner was over and the speeches started. Finally the Chinese statesman got up and made a most beautiful speech in the king's English, Oxfordian English. As he sat down he turned to the politician, "You likee speechee?"

When the Americans landed on the moon, great excitement swept throughout the world as they set up the flag. Everyone everywhere rejoiced, except in Russia. A Russian official went to the British Embassy and said, "We think it is very crass that the Americans did not put the United Nations flag on the moon. They put up their own flag and we would like you to explain to Washington that we think it was bad taste." The English Ambassador said, "Well, I'd love to do it, but I really can't. However, if you don't like the flag flying there, why don't you take it down?"

Two cavemen lived together in a cave. One caveman would make tools by grinding them on a stone, eat his meat raw and never use fire. But the second caveman, for almost everything he would use fire. He'd use fire to mold his tools and cook his meat, and the whole cave was always full of smoke. One day the first caveman said, "I can't stand it in here. All day long you have that fire going, and all that smoke is really polluting the air." And the second cave man said, "Listen, a million years from now, who's going to know the difference?"

A first sergeant in the Air Force who was in charge of billeting had a great system. If anyone was a troublemaker, he was billeted on the first floor. If someone was well behaved, he was allowed to sleep on the second floor. A new recruit came in. The sergeant said, "What's your name?" "I'm Joe Smith." "Now, son, I have a little system just to find out where people are going to live. Do you stay up late at night?" He said, "No, I'm always in bed early." "Do you go to church?" "Every Sunday." "Got any girl friends?" "Nope, just a picture of my Mom." "Do you drink?" "I don't drink." "All right," said the sergeant, "this one's a liar; put him on the first floor."

4

Tall Tales and Short . . .

Little Tommy Tucker, sang for his supper;
But he had a voice like Tiny Tim
So he didn't get much to eat.

The great Martian astronaut was told to appear before the Leader. When he did, he was told his next mission: "You are to go to Earth and bring back an earthling. Our reputation is being overshadowed by Venus, and an earthling to exhibit would be a great status builder." The Martian floated down to Earth in the middle of the Arizona desert. There by the roadside was a deserted gas station. The Martian sidled up to the nearest pump: "Take me to your Leader, please." After a bit, he asked a little more firmly, "Take me to your Leader, *please*." He asked several more times, but there was nothing more he could do, for he had two heads but no arms with which to grab. So the Martian sidled back into his spaceship and floated back to Mars to report. "Sir, I saw an earthling and I asked him several times to take me to his Leader." "What did he do?" "Nothing." "Was he hostile?" "No, he just stood there with his tail in his ear."

Noah had just filled the Ark with two of very kind of animal. Just as he was shutting the door, a man walked up and said, "Noah, you've got to let me in." Noah said, "I can't. The Ark is completely filled with every kind of insect and with birds and animals." "But you've got to let me in." Noah said, "I'm sorry," and slammed the door in his face. The man took two steps back and said, "I hope it rains."

The man couldn't sleep because he kept dreaming all night that he was awake. His friend couldn't sleep because the shade was up. He would have pulled it down, but his arm couldn't reach across the street.

In the 1968 Olympics Bob Beamon broad jumped an unbelievable 29 feet 2½ inches. The true story, of course, has never been told. Beamon was actually entered in the shotput but just as he was about to toss the metal ball he backed into a javelin thrower.

An Englishman was touring the United States with his wife. He was fascinated by the efficiency of the farmers in the midwest. He went up to one farmer and said, "I beg your pardon, sir, but I've never seen so much corn. It seems that all you have in America is corn—acres and acres of it. What do you do with all this corn?" The farmer said, "We eat what we can, and what we can't eat we can." The Englishman went back to his car and told his wife. "Remarkable chaps, these Americans. I was talking to this farmer about the corn and he said that they ate what they could and what they couldn't they could."

A song never played on the radio? "When Your Hair Has Turned to Silver, Give It to Me and I'll Hock It."

An ad: "For Sale: second-hand tombstone. A good buy for anybody named Schwartz."

> There was a young lady named Rose,
> Who had a big wart on her nose.
> When she had it removed
> Her appearance improved,
> But her glasses slipped down to her toes.

> A sheep which resided at Shotton
> For emergencies cared not a button.
> At an oncoming car

It merely said *Baaa*—
In less than two toots it was mutton.

A salesman was walking through a small Midwestern town where he didn't know anyone. An old gentleman was sitting on the porch of a hardware store, rocking, and as the salesman went by, the old gentleman said invitingly, "Howdy." So the salesman sat down in the next rocker. After ten minutes or so of silent rocking, the salesman said, "Beautiful countryside." "Certainly is. See that great big hill up there. That's where we plant our pumpkins. Biggest pumpkins in the world. Some of them may grow so huge that they can be hollowed out for families to live in." "Really? But how do they plant them up there?" "Well, about twice a year we get all the seeds and put them in shotguns and just stand on the porch here and shoot them into the hill." The salesman looked unbelieving. "Is that so? And how do you pick them?" "We don't have to pick them. Just wait until they are really getting big and ripe. Then they sort of fall off and roll all the way down the hill right into the railway station. Last year we had 27 biggies. And all the young boys are there and they load the pumpkins onto the train, and they take them to Chicago and sell them. Sold all 27 last year and got fifteen hundred dollars for 'em." "Is that a fact?" "No, that's not a fact, but it makes good conversation."

A Martian landed down on Earth and walked into a dilapidated diner. It had sawdust on the floor and was dingy and dirty. Over in the corner a jukebox was playing, its beautiful lights flickering off and on and off and on. The Martian walked over to the jukebox and said, "What's a nice girl like you doing in a joint like this?"

A Texas rancher took a little garment worker out to his big ranch.
"Look at that, I've really got a spread here. I've got so much land you could put the whole Bronx right here. And look at the cattle! In a million years, you couldn't guess how many cattle I've got out there."

The little fellow from the garment district looked and said, "You've got exactly one thousand, six hundred and eighty-two head of cattle."

The Texan said, "My gosh, that's amazing! That's exactly how many I have. How did you count them so fast?"

"Nothing to it. I count legs and divide by four."

Confucius says: "Person who eat too many sweets, take up too many seats."

Mohammed says: "Confucius talks too much."

Here is a song title dedicated to any starlet: "If You Were The Only Girl In the World, With My Luck You'd Be My Sister."

"Dear Editor: What's the best way to keep milk from going sour?"

Keep it in the cow.

"Dear Editor: Every time I make an angel food cake, someone slams the door and my cake falls. What should I do?"

If your angel food cake falls, serve it as devil's food cake.

There was an international contest to determine who had caught the biggest fish. The fellow from Canada said, "In Canada I caught a muskellunge five feet long that weighed almost a ton." And the next man got up and he said, "I caught a fish in the English Channel that was six foot two and weighed over a ton." The little man from Brooklyn got up and said, "Well, gentlemen, I caught a fish off Sheepshead Bay that was three feet." "Wait a minute, Mr. Moskavitz, the man from Canada caught one five feet long and the man from London caught one that was six-two. Why do you bother telling us about a fish only three feet long?" "In Brooklyn, we measure the fish between the eyes."

A song titled: Meet Me at the Butcher Shop, Baby, I've a Bone to Pick With You.

And is there a song titled: Be True to Your Teeth and They Won't Be False to You?

The maharaja was so wealthy he could afford to satisfy any whim. He decided on a bizarre way to give away some of his money. He threw a tremendous party and announced: "I am going to give a million dollars and half of all my gold and diamond mines, or the hand of my beautiful daughter Jarina and a dowry of her weight in rubies to some fortunate man. The choice will be his. To win this prize, the lucky man will merely have to swim from one end to the other of my pool. The pool, may I mention, is stocked with man-eating piranhas. Ready, gentlemen? . . . On your mark, get set, go!"

Every man present dove in. There were screams, gasps; and the water turned red. One lone man got out at the other end of the pool.

"Congratulations," the maharaja said. "Have you decided what you want for your prize?"

"Yes, just one thing."

"And that is. . ."

"The name of the person who pushed me in."

The astronauts had landed on the moon. As soon as they stepped out of their spaceship, they saw coming toward them an absolutely gorgeous creature . . . curvaceous, blue eyes, blonde hair, perfect measurements.

One astronaut said, "Oh, you are lovely! The most beautiful being in the solar system."

The creature replied, "Well, if you think I'm lovely, wait till you see the women."

A canny young fisher named Fisher
Once fished from the edge of a fissure.
A fish with a grin, pulled the fisherman in.
Now they are fishing the fissure for Fisher.

John Barleycorn and a friend of his were sitting on the patio when a big spaceship came down and landed right in front of them. The door opened and out came a little spaceman—all green with antennas sticking out of his ears. And his head was shaped like a corkscrew. John's friend said, "Don't you think I ought to shoot him?" But John protested, "Anybody with a head shaped like a corkscrew can't be all bad."

The title of biggest liar probably goes to a man who told people he was a diamond cutter. Really he mowed the lawn at Yankee Stadium.

A fellow went into the barbershop and said, "You know that hair restorer you sold me yesterday?" "Yeah." "I took it home and my wife didn't know what it was and she used it on all the furniture, thinking it was furniture polish." "Well, that can't do any harm." "I want to ask you something, barber. What do you charge to shave a piano?"

"Baa, baa, black sheep, have you any wool?"
"No, ma'am; ma'am."
"Well, then, I'll have to knit with nylon."

Why is English the mother tongue? Because father seldom has a chance to use it.

Mary, Mary quite contrary
How does your garden grow?
With silver bells and cockle shells
And lots and lots of fertilizer.

A song idea: "Grandpa Wanted to Start A Third Party—He Got Thrown Out of Two Last Night."

Let no one forget the immortal words of a great lion trainer when somebody asked to see one of his big cats: "I'm sorry, the lion is busy."

A drinking song: "Conductor, Let Me Off at the Next Stop; I Thought This Was the Lunch Wagon."

A song dedicated to the Department of Internal Revenue: "Oh, Leave Me Something to Remember You By."

A survey has concluded that the parking problem is becoming worse. In the old days the only parking problem was getting the girl to agree to it.

In the park there was a big bronze statue of Robert E. Lee and next to it one of the Indian chief Tecumseh. Every midnight the statues come to life. One night Tecumseh said, "General Lee, what would you do if you were alive again?" General Lee said, "I would get a gun and fill it full of buckshot." "You would like to relive the Battle of Bull Run?" "No. I'd like to kill about 40,000 of these lousy pigeons."

Let us celebrate the birthday of Sam Sulphur, the man who invented the match. Without this marvelous invention, to start a fire you would have to rub two Boy Scouts together.

The National Safety Council warns that alcohol and gasoline don't mix. Oh, they're so wrong. They do mix, but they taste terrible.

The little fruit boat was loaded with oranges. It also carried a couple of passengers, one of whom was a loud-mouthed salesman. Suddenly the boat was attacked by a monstrous whale. The crew tossed crates full of oranges overboard to appease it, but still the whale humped and bumped the little boat, almost overturning it. Then someone thought of the obnoxious salesman—tossing him overboard might satisfy the whale and it would certainly get rid of the salesman. The crew threw the salesman overboard and the whale swam away. A couple of days later, the little boat made it to land. There beached on the shore, was the whale. Standing inside its open mouth was the salesman: "Get your fresh oranges right here . . ."

Let us not forget the immortal words of Josephine, who said to Napoleon, "If you are going to Russia, I don't care what you say, take your galoshes."

Once upon a time there were two cement mixers and they got married. And now there's a little sidewalk running around the house.

The man's name was Ferris. He was a big wheel.

"City Council Bans Motorist Hornblowing."
They must be afraid the pedestrians may get away.

"U.S. Treasury Department announces that the new dollar will last nine months."
That's nice—most dollars usually last about three minutes.

"Man Accidentally Swallows Car Keys." Poor man, he probably had to walk home!

A song for Grandmother's Day: "Don't Go Into the Stable, Grandmother—You're Too Old to Be Horsing Around."

A native of Maine was visiting New York. As he stood on the corner watching the people go up and down Broadway, a man said to him, "Hey, you must be new in town. How do you like this cold weather?" "I don't think it's so cold." "You don't think it's cold," said the New Yorker. "Why, it's 3 below zero." "Have you ever been to Maine?" "Yeah, I've been to Maine." "Have you ever been to Barnaby Square?" "Yeah, I've been to Barnaby Square." "Well, you know that statue they've got in the middle of Barnaby Square?" "You mean the statue of Lincoln?" "Yes, the statue of Lincoln with his hands on the little boy's shoulder. Well, when I left there yesterday and it was so cold, Lincoln had taken his hands off the boy's shoulder and put them in his pockets."

A disk jockey is a man who lives on spins and needles.

> There was a young girl in the choir,
> Whose voice went higher and higher.
> One Sunday night
> It vanished from sight,
> And they found it next day in the spire.

Let us not forget the famous words of Mrs. Santa Claus who said on December 24: "I don't care where you're going tonight, I need the sleigh and the reindeer."

Pony Express is a game like Post Office but it moves faster.

There are signs on hotel doors that read: "Have You Left Anything?"
Well, the Internal Revenue office has a sign on its door that reads: "Have You Anything Left?"

A sign on a store read: "Wanted: Man Who Wo
Eight Hours a Day, to Replace Man Who Doesn't."

It's so silly the way they put ads in the paper, withou
punctuation: For sale a house by lady with red brick front
and purple door.

An ad: Bloodhound for sale. What am I offered for a one-year-old, beautiful animal, good watch dog? Will eat anything, especially fond of children.

> There lived a thin maid named Lena
> Who bought a new vacuum cleaner.
> She got in the way
> Of the suction one day
> And since then nobody has seen her.

Let us not forget Abraham Lincoln, who may have said, "Someday they're going to name a tunnel between New York and New Jersey after me and they're going to call it the Abraham Tunnel."

One way to get over having trouble going to sleep the night before a trip is to leave a day earlier.

Reverend Gatemound decided that he'd take a vacation in the Dakotas and do a little bear hunting. As he walked through the wilds, his shoe lace came undone. He placed his trusty rifle against a rock and knelt down on one knee to tie his shoe. When he was about to stand up, he looked up and there right in front of him, right between him and his rifle, was 750 pounds of grizzly bear. Well, he couldn't get to his gun, that was sure; so he stayed where he was and said; "While I'm down here I might as well do a good job. Lord, it looks like my time has come. Lord, I think that I have always lived the way that you have wanted me to live and, if this is truly the end, please let it be swift and painless. But, Lord, if by some strange quirk of fate, I am to win out over this mighty beast, let me strike swiftly in a humane death. If it happens that you are undecided, sit right down here on this stump and watch one of the wildest fights you have ever seen."

A song title: "Get Out of The Wheat Fields, Grandma, You're Going Against the Grain."

A song: "She Was Only a Shoemaker's Daughter, But She Went Out With All the Heels."

A song title: "I Was Out With My Girl Last Night And the Moon Was Yellow, and I Was a Little Chicken Myself."

Dedicated to a teacher: "She May Be a Schoolteacher's Daughter, But She Certainly Has No Class."

The driver of a beat-up Volkswagon pulled up alongside a great big beautiful chauffeur-driven Rolls Royce. He paced himself so he could stay alongside and really take a good look at that classic of a car. He envied the man sitting back on the passenger seat and reading a paper. The Volkswagon driver saw a little light start flashing and the passenger reach over and pick up a phone. "Wow, what luxury," he thought to himself. Suddenly the man in the Rolls Royce leaned over, spoke to the chauffeur, who pushed a button and the rear window rolled down. The man shoved the phone toward the Volkswagon driver and said, "It's for you."

One girl was so skinny that three times in one week a dog tried to bury her in the backyard.

They were the first two men to land on Mars. One of them had to stay in the space capsule while the other went outside to gather samples of Mars rocks. When his speciman bags were full, he plodded back to the capsule, climbed the ladder, and knocked on the hatch to be let in. "All right, just a minute. Who's there?"

All night the man dreamed he was playing cards and shooting dice. He just rolled and tossed all night.

Theme song for a salesman's convention: "No One Has Endurance Like the Man Who Sells Insurance."

> There was a young girl from St. Paul
> Who wore a newspaper dress to a ball.
> The dress caught on fire
> And burnt her entire
> Front page, sports section and all.

A Texan walked into Club 21 in New York and announced proudly, "My wife has just given birth to a baby boy. The nurse just called me from Houston. She tells me it's the biggest boy ever been born to any woman in the whole world. Drinks for everyone. The nurse told me the bed sheets they're using are 81 by 109." The gentleman next to him said, "That happens to be the usual double-bed sheet size." "Yeah, but we're using them for diapers."

> There was a young lady of Kent
> Whose nose was most awfully bent.
> She followed her nose
> One day, I suppose,
> And no one knows which way she went.

On a rainy night, the traveling salesman's car broke down. He made his way through the rain until he finally found a house. He knocked. The door was opened by an old man: "What do you want?" "I'm a traveling salesman. My car broke down. Could I spend the night?" The old man said, "Come right in and sit down by the fire. You are welcome to stay overnight." Nobody lives here but me." The salesman said, "Oh, oh, excuse me, but I got to go." "What's the matter?" "I'm in the wrong joke."

It had been raining in this Midwestern town until everything was a sea of mud. If Noah's ark had been available everyone would have gotten out of town. But there was no ark building going on, and the best the inhabitants could do was joke about it. Mrs. Noah was said to have said to her husband after all the animals were in the ark, "I told you to put newspapers on the floor." This town was so muddy that walking in the streets was an adventure. One man saw a silk hat moving along in the mud. So he lifted it, and there was a head under it. He apologized for taking off any man's hat: "But you must be really in the mud." "Heck," came the answer, "I'm riding a horse."

> There was a young lady named Kate
> Who was learning on rollers to skate.
> Her friends for a game
> Quickly gave her a name:
> Niagara—her falls were so great.

An avid fisherman who went to the West Indies to fish

every winter vacation invited his West Indian fishing-boat captain to Maine one summer. They went up into the North Woods to the New Englander's favorite lake. All morning the West Indian kept pulling out fish while his host caught absolutely nothing. This went on every day for almost a week. The New Englander was getting bothered, so very early the following morning he sneaked out, took his friend's tackle and very quietly rowed out on the lake. Very carefully he cast his line and waited. Nothing happened. Just as he was about to row back to shore, a barracuda stuck his head out of the water and said, "Hey, where's José?"

A lady once said, "You have to go to Africa to see a man-eating lion, but you have to go to a delicatessen to see a man eating herring."

Why is a bigamist like a drunken driver?
Because they both had one too many.

A wonderful line is that of an old friend of Socrates: "A friend in need is a pest."

A Texan and a Californian were talking. The Californian said, "Do you know, in California our orange trees have to have great big funnels under them so that when an orange falls, it drops into the funnel, and the juice goes straight to the cannery. If we didn't have these funnels the groves would be flooded."

"Well, in Texas the sun is strong and beautiful. I had an uncle that had a cornfield where the corn grew so big that one time, on one ear of corn, I saw 19 crows resting comfortably and each and every one of those 19 crows was eating as fast as he could."

Later that year they both got drafted. They met again in the front line with shells coming down all around them. Both the Texan and the Californian realized they might not live through this.

The Californian said, "I want to tell you that everything

I told you about the orange groves in California was a lie. I don't want to die with a lie on my conscience."

The Texan said, "In that case, I have to tell you that I, too, exaggerated a little. The 19th crow was not resting comfortably on that ear of corn. He was standing on one foot."

One hunter was showing another his trophy room, "I think the most thrilling hunt I've ever been on was a safari I went on with my uncle last year. That's when I bagged that huge lion you see in the corner, probably the world's largest. Didn't even have to stuff him." "You didn't? He looks stuffed." "Oh, he is—my uncle, you know."

Two friends were talking about fishing. One said, "We were just off the Baha Peninsula when we hooked a sailfish that we had to fight for seven days and nights. We fought him, and we finally got him in and gaffed him, and when we weighed him, he weighed 1,432 pounds." The other fisherman said, "I was down near that Baha Peninsula just a few weeks ago, and we had a similar experience. We hooked a fish, and it took us thirteen days and nights to bring in this fantastic creature. And when we brought this creature up, to gaff him, it wasn't a fish at all. It was the binnacle of an old Spanish galleon and, would you believe it, there right in the top of that old binnacle the light was still on." His friend looked at him and said, "I'll tell you, I'll take 1,200 pounds off my fish, if you'll put out that light in the binnacle."

Immigration men are knowledgable. They are pretty clever guys. This one fellow in particular has a little trick. He asks: "What's your nationality?" "American." "American, huh? Do you know the words of the *Star Spangled Banner?*" "No, I don't." "You're an American, go in."

The farmers in the area had been having a deal of trouble with crows stealing their seed corn. One farmer explained how he had solved the problem: he put up the most hideous scarecrow imaginable. Not only was it horrifying to look at, but it made noises and flapped its arms. His neighbor admitted it looked frightening, but did the crows know it? "Are you kidding? The crows are so scared they just brought back corn they stole three years ago."

The girl was so skinny, that, when she put on a fur coat, she looked like a pipe cleaner.

The world's skinniest kid is the girl who was so thin that if she stood sideways she was marked absent. If she took a nickel out of her pocket, it threw her off balance.

A nosy friend kept asking, "Where are you going on your vacation?" "I don't know." "Going to Greece or one of those places to see the old ruins?" "Nope." "Going to Italy to see the old ruins?" "Nope." "Going to Egypt to see the old Ruins?" "Nope, I think I'll go to Paris and see the young ruins."

The greatest argument of all times is probably the legendary Hatfield-McCoy feud. One big battle went on for two or three days. Afterward one of the Hatfields dragged out of the river was found to have 85 bullet holes in him. And one of the McCoys walked over, looked over the corpse and said to the sheriff standing there, "Worst case of suicide I ever saw."

When one of George Bernard Shaw's plays opened, he sent a telegram to Winston Churchill. With his rather caustic Irish wit, he telegraphed: "You are invited to the opening night of my new play. Here are two tickets. Bring a friend, if any."

Churchill replied: "I cannot attend the opening night of your play; please send me tickets for the second night, if any."

Most orchestra conductors are a bit eccentric, not necessarily crazy, but tending to long hair and marked idiosyncrasies. This great old Italian conductor who was in his 90's always looked at his cuffs. One night at a concert in Rome, he had a heart attack while he was conducting and collapsed on the podium. The members of the orchestra rushed to help him. One of the musicians noticed his cuffs. On them was written: "Flutes to the left. Violins to the right."

A teacher in Siberia was having a lot of trouble having the students understand and talk English. "I want you to know that I am leaving soon. You all have been so terribly stubborn, you haven't even tried to learn." A student in the back of the room protested: "I, ah, happen to speak the English very well. I think you should not say these things and include all in us. I can say in the English language "come here," and the person I speak will come here." The teacher said, "That's all very well, but suppose you want someone to go there." The student said, "Ah, well, if I someone want to go there, I go there and say, 'Come here.' "

5

There Were These Two . . .

I have a very important message for those people who were born under Taurus the Bull. You can come out now.

Two Texans named Jack and Howard lunched together at a club. When they left the club, they walked down the street together past a Rolls Royce showroom. Jack said, "Howard, come on in here." Inside, Jack called the salesman over and asked, "Boy, how much is that Rolls Royce, the gold one?" "Thirty seven thousand dollars, sir." "We'll take two of them." Jack reached into his pocket and pulled out a wad, but Howard protested, "Wait a minute, Jack. You paid for lunch, let me take this."

In the old West where gamblers were rough and tough, it was nothing to get into an argument over gambling and shoot someone if he cheated. Then law and order came to the wild West and they didn't do it that way any more. If gamblers fell out, they had to go to court. In one case, a man accused another of cheating at cards. "How can you be so certain that he cheated?"asked the judge. The man said, "I'm absolutely positive." "But how do you know?" He wasn't playing the hand I dealt him."

This fellow was broke. He was always gambling, and he never had any money. In Vegas one time, he recognized a friend, "Rosie, you've got to loan me $200." Rosie felt sorry for him, so she gave him the money. The next time she was in Vegas, he was there again. He said, "Listen, I haven't forgotten that I owe you three hundred dollars." "You borrowed only two hundred." "Well, it's going to be three hundred."

Two cons were walking in the prison yard. One asked, "What are you in for?"

"Murder."

"How long did you get?"

"Ninty-nine years."

"What are you going to do when you get out?"

"I don't know, go somewhere where I'm not known, and start all over again."

A conscienceless con man had bilked an old lady out of a lot of money, and with it rented a huge suite. It was truly an exquisite place. On the door he had printed: "Well Known Business Investor Company, Inc." As he was admiring the decor, he heard someone coming down the corridor. The person stopped outside his door. Aha, he figured, a sucker. When the man came in, there was the con man talking on the phone: "Yeah, uhhuh, well, listen, $450,000 might be all right but, believe you me, I would not do it for half a million. If you don't want to do it for that the deal's off. . . . What do I care? It was $200,000 yesterday and $400,000 the day before. . . . Why do I need you? . . . Well, OK." He hung up and turned to the man who had come in: "Yes, what can I do for you?" "Can't do a thing. I am here to hook up your phone."

Two horse players went to the racetrack and one said, "I'm just going to place a bet." About twenty minutes later his friend saw him, looking exhausted. "What's the matter with you?" "Are you kidding? I went to place a bet. I was at the two dollar window, and I dropped my money. I bent down to pick it up and a guy threw a blanket over me and another guy came up and put a saddle over me, and a jockey got on my back." "So what?" "So what! Didn't you see me? I came in third."

At the big circus in Madison Square Garden, the ringmaster stood in the middle of the sawdust floor of the center ring and announced: "And now, ladies and gentlemen, we are very proud to present our main attraction, the Great Moe Noodleman. He will climb to the top of this 80-foot wooden pole and jump into this vat of hot tea. Ladies and gentlemen, the one and only Moe Noodleman." The performer, wrapped up in a raccoon coat, walked across the sawdust to the 80-foot pole, and started laboriously climbing hand over hand. As he climbed it became obvious that he was rather aged. Finally he got to the top, threw off the coat, looked at the audience and said, "Ladies and gentlemen, my name is Moe Noodleman. I am 79 years old. Do you want me to jump off the top of this 80-foot pole, into that vat of hot tea?" Everybody looked up at him and down at the vat of tea: "No, no . . . no . . . no . . ." Moe Noodleman bowed and said, "Thank you. The next show will be at nine thirty."

A friend of mine asked me, "Where can I go for my holiday? I think I'll go to Mexico." I said, "Don't go there; go to Sardinia or Corsica. They are marvelous places." So off he went. About four or five weeks later, I saw him in Beverly Hills. I said, "How are you?" He said, "Well, you're a great one. You remember what you told me, you idiot? Go to Sardinia, go to Corsica and have a great time in the sun. I was there sixteen days, and it rained in the morning, in the afternoon and in the evening and sometimes during the night. The sun never shone." I looked at him: "I don't understand—you're brown, you have a great suntan." "This is not a suntan, you idiot. It's rust."

Aristocracy is a wonderful thing with its titles and glamour but sometimes even the upper classes are in financial difficulty. This particular Earl was speaking with his secretary, Heathcliffe. Heathcliffe said, "Your Grace, you owe fifty pounds to the green grocer." The Earl replied, "Promise him twenty pounds." Heathcliffe added, "But also you owe a hundred to the tailor." The Earl replied, "Promise him eighty." "You owe the chemist thirty pounds two shillings and tuppence." The Earl said, "Promise him ten pounds." And as the Earl walked out for his usual ride with the hounds, he added quickly, "Oh, Heathcliffe, promise yourself something, too."

Two very drunk men hailed a cab in Los Angeles: "Cabbie, I want you to take my friend and me to 76th Street." "There's no 76th Street in L.A." "Who said L.A? We want to go to 76th Street in New York." "If you want to go to New York, you should go by train, bus or plane. It's too expensive to hire a cab for that trip." "Oh yeah? What do you call expensive?" "At least $2,000." One of the drunks took out a whole bundle of hundred dollar bills, and counted out $2,000: "Here you are. Your $2,000 and a couple of hundred for a tip, now take us to 76th Street in New York . . ." Then he turned to his friend and said, "Get in." "No, you get in first." "Oh, come on, you get in first. You know I get out at 64th Street."

The two fellows were discussing their jobs, trying to determine who had the more unusual occupation. One fellow said, "I have a really odd job. I'm in the shoo business." And the other said, "I don't like to argue with you, but I don't see what is so odd about that. Millions of people sell shoes." "Oh, no, you don't understand. I don't *sell* shoes. You see, I work for an insect-repellent company, and it's my job to go from house to house wherever they have flies and mosquitos and that sort of thing. I run around and say, 'Shoo, shoo, shoo.' "

This fellow took an ocean trip but he didn't enjoy it: "Next vacation I'm going to see America." The following year he got into his car and drove all over, taking pictures everywhere. Finally he came home and went into a little photo store. "Do you make life-size enlargements from snapshots?"

The fellow said, "Yes, I do." "Well, here, I took some shots of the Grand Canyon."

He had bought one of these English cars. He kept careful records for a month because everybody said the mileage was so sensational. Obviously he wasn't getting what he was supposed to be getting. So he took the car to the mechanic and told him to check it out. The car was in perfect condition. The owner protested, "Look, I love this car, but evidently I am not getting the mileage that I am supposed to be getting." The mechanic looked at him and said, "Why don't you do what all the other foreign car owners do?" "What's that?" "Lie about it."

A clergyman took over a church that looked like a war relic—windows broken; plaster fallen; pews moth-eaten. In his very first sermon he said, "My brothers and sisters, I take a look around here, and see ruin. We've all got to get together and raise a fund to restore this building to the beautiful shrine it once was. I want to hear your donations. I want you to pledge money." Suddenly a little old fellow, who was known all over town as the stingiest of men, said, "I'd like to start off with a donation of $5." Just then a bit of plaster fell down and hit him on the head. The miser said, "Maybe I should make that $50." A voice from the back pleaded, "Hit him one more time, Lord."

Two bums were brought before the judge on a vagrancy charge. The judge looked down at the ragged pair and addressed himself to the one standing on the right, "Tell me your name and address." "My name's Joe Johnson, and I live under the stars and beneath the trees, in the beautiful woods on this beautiful earth. That's where I live." The judge turned to the other bum, "And what's your name and address?" "Sam Fritz, and I live next door to him."

Two Indians were watching vacationers waterskiing on a lake near their reservation.

One Indian asked, "Why man drive boat so fast?"
The other answered, "Little man on string chase him."

A play opened on Broadway, and it was dreadful. The producer went through all the papers looking for the write-ups. He read maybe five or six of the most important critics on Broadway—no mention of his play. He finally reached one critic on the phone. "I looked through all the paper, and I didn't find your review of my play. I know you were there. You saw the play; how come you didn't write anything?" "I didn't know how to spell p-p-pft."

Two women who hadn't seen each other in a couple of years met on the street. One said, "Hello! And how's it been going with you?" The other said, "It's been going very well. I'm extremely wealthy, you know. My husband went into another business, and we have so much money we don't know what to do with it." "That's fantastic." "Yes, my daughter married a very wealthy doctor—he's an eye specialist—and he makes money hand over fist." The other woman said, "That's fantastic." "Yes, and of course I have so many furs and jewels I don't know what to do with them. We've got a house in Rome and a house in Vienna and a house in Paris." "That's fantastic." "And how are things with you?" "Well, my husband is driving a cab, but we're getting along pretty good. My daughter married a school teacher. He's a very nice upstanding young man, and that's about it. As for me, I don't do much with my time except go to charm school." "Oh, what do you learn there?" "For one thing, I learn to say 'Fantastic' instead of 'You're full of baloney.'"

The two men were sitting in the Playboy Club arguing about the art of making love. One said, "The art of making love is 50% pleasure and 50% work." The other disagreed, "Making love is 60% work and 40% pleasure." The two almost came to blows before they decided that the only way to settle the argument was to get another opinion. They decided that they would ask the first person that passed by, and whatever his answer was, it would settle the argument. Just then, Willie Rush, the bus boy, came by. They grabbed him. "Look, you've got to settle a bet. I say that making love is 50% pleasure and 50% work. He says that making love is 60% work and 40% pleasure. What do you say?" And Willie looked at both of them and said, "I think you're both wrong. If there were any work involved in it, you would probably have me doing it."

The 99-pound weakling was down on the beach the other day, talking to his girl when a 185-pound bully came up and kicked some sand in his face. What could he do? He sent away for a course, a course of muscle-building exercises that really make you strong and handsome. Believe it or not, in a matter of seven weeks he was in beautiful shape. He weighed 212 pounds, and had rippling muscles. He went down on the beach and a 380-pound bully kicked sand in his face.

This young fellow was in a tearing hurry to make a train. He thought he could make it if he took all the short-cuts, such as running catty-corner across the farmer's field. To be polite, he decided he should ask permission of the farmer, who was coming around from behind the barn, "Do you mind if I dash across your field? I've got to make the 6:30 train." "Go right ahead. If my bull sees you, you'll make the 6:00."

Every time the driver of the sports car tried to pass, the truck driver ahead of him pulled into the middle of the road and the man in the sports car had to drop back and over to the right again. For twenty miles the driver of the sports car honked and signalled, but the truck driver would not let him pass. Finally, at the end of twenty miles, the truck pulled into a gas station. The sports car pulled right up alongside. The truck driver rolled down his window. He was tough. "Go ahead, say it. I'd just like to hear what you think of me." And the driver of the sports car looked up and answered, "I know what I think of you. I was just curious to see what one looked like."

A man running as fast as he could down the street was stopped by an acquaintance, "Wait a minute, why are you running?"

"I'm running to stop a fight."

"Who's fighting?"

"Me and another guy."

Two friends who hadn't seen each other in a while met on the street. One said, "Hey, I've got a fantastic joke for you." "What is it?" "These two Jewish guys are walking down the street . . ." "Wait a minute, every time you tell me a joke it's two Jewish guys walking down the street. I'm sick of them. Don't you know any other kind of joke?" "Sure. Two Chinamen were walking down the street and one says, to the other, 'So listen, what are you going to do come Yom Kippur?' "

An English actor who was very prone to boasting about everything he did came to America. After doing some work over here, he returned to England. He met a friend on the street one day, and the friend asked, "How did you do in America?" "Marvelously. Of course you know I was with the Shakespeare repertoire company in Central Park. I opened as King Lear and everything was marvelous. In the third act, I actually had the audience glued to their seats." "How marvelous of you to think of that device."

Two women went to the movies and one of them started to cough. Her friend leaned away from her. The more she coughed, the farther her friend tried to move away. Finally the cougher turned around to her friend and said, "Look, you don't have to move away like that. This is not a sickness." And the other woman said, "Well, it ain't a wellness."

The defendant in an assault and battery case was on the stand. The prosecutor said, "What I want to know is, how hard did you push the plaintiff?" "I just pushed him a little bit, sir." "How hard?" "Just a little bit." The prosecutor walked over to his assistant and said, "I think I have him badly rattled. I shall ask him to demonstrate how hard he pushed, and I shall ask him to push me. I'm sure he'll over-do it and we'll win the case." He turned to the judge and said, "Your Honor, I would like the defendant to come down here and demonstrate how hard he pushed my client." The man got down, walked over to the prosecutor and, pow!, knocked him down. Then he jumped on the prosecutor, kicked him, bit him, picked him up and threw him right across the table. The defendant turned to the judge and said, "Uh, it was about one-tenth that hard, your Honor."

The Sicilian had brought along a group of his friends, for it was a big, big day—he was going to become an American citizen. The examining judge said, "My boy, I am going to ask you a few questions to see what you know of the history of our land. Who was the first President of the United States?" The Sicilian smiled and answered, "The first President of the United States was George Washington." All his friends shouted, "Thata boy! Thata boy!" "Remember now, you're in a courtroom. That's correct. Now question number two: Who made the first American flag?" "The first American flag was made by Betsy Ross." "Yeah! Thata boy." "Quiet! Who killed Abraham Lincoln?" The Sicilian thought for a while and finally he said, "I don't know." A voice from the back called out, "Thata boy, Tony, don't squeal."

A director walked into a movie producer's office, picked up a script and quickly put it down. He said, "Are you kidding? What are you doing anyway? This is the worst piece of trash I have ever seen." "I don't understand, you looked only at the title." "It's the title that's the worst thing about it. It's 'The Optimist.'" "Right." "What sort of title is that? *You* know what optimist means, I know what optimist means, but how many of those hamburgers out front will know the story is about an eye doctor?"

An Irishman and a Dutchman were having a terrible argument. They decided to step outside and settle it with their fists, like gentlemen. Just as they were squaring off for their fight, a college student stepped forward and said, "Hey, since there's no referee, why don't you just scrap until one of you has had enough and then yells loud, 'Sufficient.' Whoever yells it out, the other will be the winner." The Dutchman and Irishman agreed: "That is a sensational idea." So they fought. They punched, pushed and kicked for at least an hour and a half. By this time they were both in bad shape, and the Dutchman said, "Ah, sufficient." And the Irishman said, "Thank goodness! I've been trying to think of that word for the last half hour."

The plaintiff was extremely near-sighted. Though he was sure that the accused was the man who had picked his pocket, he could not swear to a positive identification. Since there was no other evidence against the prisoner, the judge could only declare him not guilty and free him. But the man made no move to go. Everyone else cleared out of the courtroom but he still hung around. The judge said, "You are free to go now." The fellow just shuffled from one foot to the other. The judge said, "You've been declared not guilty, so you don't have to stay." After a few minutes' thought, the man said, "Your honor, does all this mean that I can keep the watch?"

A drunk in a bar was having an argument with another customer, "I heard what you said, and I'm going to give you just five seconds to take that back or you're in big trouble." "Yeah? And what if I don't take the five seconds?" And the drunk answered, "Well, how much time do you want?"

A braggart walked into a bar. He looked at pictures on the walls of Joe Louis and Rocky Marciano and Jack Dempsey: "Bums. Nothin' but bums. They couldn't fight. I can beat any of 'em. Because I'm a lion. And they call me the Lion of Detroit." A little runt of a man was standing next to him at the bar, and all of a sudden the little runt hit the boaster right in the stomach. He fell flat on the floor. As he got up, he said, "I want to tell you something . . . There's one thing you should never do. You must not hit a lion in the stomach."

An Englishman was walking through a small Mexican village. He realized that he had left his watch in the hotel and had no way to tell the time. The whole square was deserted except for one peasant having a little siesta. Dozing next to him was his burro. The Englishman walked over and asked, "I'm terribly sorry to trouble you, but can you tell me the correct time?" The Mexican opened his eyes and said, "Si, señor." He lifted the burro's tail and said, "It's ten o'clock," and went back to sleep. The Englishman thanked him and walked away, thinking about the extraordinary way the Mexican had of telling the time. After a while the Englishman decided, to go back and asked the Mexican how he had done it. The Mexican peasant was still there, dozing with his burro beside him. "Pardon me," the Englishman said, "but can you tell me the correct time?" The Mexican opened his eyes, lifted the burro's tail and said, "Si, señor. It is seven minutes past ten." "Thank you. I hope you won't think I'm being rude, but would you mind telling me how you tell the time by lifting up your burro's tail?" "It is very simple, señor. When I lift the burro's tail, I can see the clock across the street."

A Scotsman on vacation in Atlantic City was walking along the pier with his little son. All of a sudden the boy fell off the pier into the water. Everyone started screaming. The lifeguard dove in, swam around until he found the drowning boy and dragged him to shore. There he gave him artificial respiration and revived him. The Scotsman ran over, crying, "Are you the lifeguard that pulled my boy out of the water, and risked his life to dive into the breakers to save his life?" "Yes, sir." "Can I ask you something? What did you do with his hat?"

The three monks had taken vows of silence. They had the right to say one sentence each, in order, one year apart. Every morning at breakfast they sat and ate in silence. One year went by and the first monk looked up and said, "I hate oatmeal." Another year went by and the second monk had his chance to speak and he said, "I love oatmeal." Another year went by, and the third monk had his turn to speak. He looked up and said, "I'm sick and tired of this constant bickering about oatmeal."

Four hunters booked a cabin in the mountains. When they got there they found it had only two rooms instead of the four they had been promised. They had a problem: Joe was a snorer, a famous snorer. The others decided to cut cards to determine who would sleep in the room with Joe. The loser showed up the next morning exhausted. "Joe snored all night like a buzz saw, and I couldn't sleep a wink." The next night they cut cards again. Another man lost, and he, too, came to breakfast exhausted. The following night the remaining hunter offered to sleep in the same room with Joe. He came to the breakfast table chipper and singing merrily. "Do you really feel like you look?" "Sure. Great. Marvelous." "You mean to tell us Joe's snoring didn't keep you awake?" "Well, I just waited until we were ready to get into bed, then I leaned over and gave him a hug and a kiss. He sat up all night watching me."

A gentleman taking his first ocean voyage to Europe, went to the dining room for breakfast. He was seated next to a Frenchman. The Frenchman nodded to him, he nodded back, and the Frenchman said, "Bon appetit." The little man answered, "Ginzburg." They had a lovely breakfast. Ginzburg wandered around the deck, until lunchtime. At lunch, they smiled at each other; the Frenchman said, "Bon appetit"; he answered, "Ginzburg." This went on day after day, and the little man became annoyed. He told an acquaintance, "I don't even know if I'm going to go to lunch today. I sit with a maniac." "What do you mean?" "A French guy. I walk in and we sit down, and every meal he tells me his name is Bon Appetit and I say Ginzburg. He always forgets, I guess." "Bon appetit means enjoy your meal; that's not his name. It's a charming French saying." Mollified, Ginzburg went in to lunch. The Frenchman was there, so Ginzburg said, "Bon appetit." And the Frenchman stood up and said, "Ginzburg."

A Texan went on a guided tour in Italy. At the Sistine Chapel, the guide pointed out the beauty of Michelangelo's famed ceiling. The Texan looked at it and said, "In Dallas we send out Christmas cards with better pictures than that." When the tour went through the Coliseum, the Texan wanted to know if anyone there had seen SMU. Just as the tour reached Mount Vesuvius, the volcano erupted. "Wow, that is something," the Texan said, "but if the Dallas fire department were here, they'd have that fire out in five minutes."

Three shipwrecked men were on a raft. The only thing they had left to eat was a huge hunk of salami. One of the men said, "We've got to work this out so there is a fair share of salami for all." Another said, "There's not enough to share. We have to think of a fair way to choose one person to get it all. Then that one person will be here when a boat comes along. The person who eats that salami will be alive." The three thought about it and one man said, "I've got it! We'll go to sleep tonight and we'll all dream. In the morning we'll tell each other our dreams and the one who has had the most bizarre dream can have the salami." When they woke up in the morning, the first man said, "I dreamed that we had been at sea for about a month when I passed away. I went up to heaven and St. Peter looked at me and said, 'Welcome, old friend' and he gave me a harp and wings." The second man said, "I had a very similar dream. We'd been floating around for months and I passed away. I went to heaven and St. Peter gave me a gown and some wings and a diamond studded harp." "Well, I went to sleep last night and I had a dream that both of you had died and gone to heaven to see St. Peter. So as you were both gone, I got up and ate the salami."

A little prospector wearing clean new clothes walked into a saloon. A big Texan said to his friend standing at the bar, "Watch me make this dude dance." He walked over to the prospector and said, "You're a foreigner, aren't you? From the East?"

"You might say that," the little prospector answered. "I'm from Boston and I'm here prospecting for gold."

"Now tell me something. Can you dance?"

"No, sir. I never did learn to dance."

"Well, I'm going to teach you. You'll be surprised how quickly you can learn."

With that, the Texan took out his gun and started shooting at the prospector's feet. Hopping, skipping, jumping, by the time the little prospector made it to the door he was shaking like a leaf.

About an hour later the Texan left the saloon. As soon as he stepped outside the door, he heard a click. He looked around and there, four feet from his head, was the biggest rifle he had ever seen.

And the little prospector said, "Mr. Texan, have you ever kissed a mule?"

"No," said the quick thinking Texan, "but I've always wanted to."

A hunter had been lost in the jungles for three days. He was hungry and weary, and getting scared that he would never find his way out. Suddenly he caught a glimpse of someone among the bushes. It was an old friend! The hunter ran toward him, crying, "John, it's me! It's me! Thank God, you've found me!" "Don't bug me—I've been lost for two weeks."

The basketball coach was depressed; his team never won. One day he was having lunch with another basketball coach and he asked, "How come your team always wins and mine always loses?" The other coach says, "I don't really know if it has anything to do with it, but I happen to be a very religious man. I am tremendously enthused about the game, and I work with my players. But I also spend a great deal of time before every game in church. And I pray for victory. Apparently someone up there is listening, because we always win. Why don't you try it?" Some weeks later the religious-minded coach met his friend again. He asked, "How are things going now?" "We're still losing every game." "Are you doing what I told you I did?" "Yes, I go to church before every game, but we keep losing." "What church are you going to?" "The one on Forty-fifth and Fifth." "That one is for horse players."

A rich Texan and his friend were walking down the street toward their cars. As they passed a Rolls Royce agency, the Texan said, "I just remembered that I have to make a phone call. Excuse me a minute." He ran into the Rolls Royce agency. About 25 minutes later, he came out. "Sorry. I don't like to keep anybody waiting, but you know how it is. While I was in there I bought another Rolls Royce." "Another Rolls Royce! What's the matter with you, you've got nine Rolls Royces now. Why did you buy another one?" "Well, you can't just use a fellow's phone without buying something."

Two friends were talking about how lucky they thought their mutual friends were. One said, "I tell you that Fred is too much. He really is. He goes to Vegas every weekend and always comes home a winner. Pays for the hotel, pays for the food. Always a winner." And the other said, "That's not so great. What about Frank? Every poker game he's a winner. Goes to the track every other day—daily doubles, everything." "Hold it. Ted is the luckiest man alive." "What makes you say that?" "Well, I'll tell you. Ted's got a wife and a cigarette lighter, and they both work."

A man couldn't get a reservation on any plane to go to Europe, and he was very nervous about boats. As soon as he boarded the liner, he started bothering the captain. He'd constantly buttonhole the captain and say, "Captain, are we going to be safe? Is everything going to be all right?" "Don't worry, I've made this crossing for years." But the man kept pestering the captain, and the captain was getting sick of it. One day, the man woke up to find they were in the middle of the worst storm in history. It took him twenty minutes to get to the bridge. He opened the door and said, "Captain, this storm is frightening me." "You don't have to worry. We're quite safe. We're within one mile of land." "Oh, that's great. Which direction?" "Straight down."

At a motion picture theater a man was hissing all the love scenes and talking continously to the screen. Annoyed, the woman sitting behind him tapped the man on the shoulder and said, "Would you please be quiet. I'm trying to watch the picture." The man was quiet for a little while, but soon he was again hissing the love scenes and carrying on. The woman finally leaned forward and tapped his shoulder, "If you're not quiet, I'm going to have the usher take you out." At this point the man turned to her indignantly and said, "Madam, I don't go out with ushers."

An Israeli was visiting in Texas and his Texan host was showing him around the ranch. "I got a mighty big ranch here. I got 40,000 head of cattle, and this ranch of mine is so big that sometimes I get into my car in the morning, and I start riding across my property, and it's like nine at night before I get to the other side." The fellow from Israel looked up and said, "To tell you the truth, I have a rotten car like that myself."

Talking about a mutual friend, the two friends agreed: "Joe is the luckiest; he goes to the track every day and he always wins." One day they cornered Joe and asked, "How come you always win?" "I think all the time. Everything is a little good luck omen to me. Like the other night. For that night and two or three nights in a row I kept dreaming about the numbers two and five. So I went out to the track and I bet on number eight, and I won." "Wait a minute—two and five is seven." "Oh," Joe said, "you got the education. I got the money."

A business man went to Formosa. After he finished his

business, for relaxation, he decided to find a poker game. Sure enough he found a poker game, but he couldn't speak Chinese and the Chinese couldn't speak English. Finally they found an interpreter. He said to the interpreter, "I'd be very grateful if you can help me." "Don't worry about a thing, sir." Everything started off smoothly. Suddenly, the American was dealt a four-card flush. He looked at it—ace, king, queen, jack of hearts. So he bet $100. And the first Chinese gentleman next to him bet "Ah loy." "What's that?" The interpreter explained: "He's raising you two." "Oh." So everybody put in two. The next Chinese gentleman said, "Ah moy." "What's 'ah moy'?" "He's betting you three hundred." "Wow," the American said, "stakes are going up." The next Chinese gentleman said, "Ah foy." "What does that mean?" The interpreter said, "He's betting you three more." The American thought the price of poker was really high in Formosa, but he put in his money and waited for the next card. He squeezed it and looked at it and looked at it, and finally he said, "Ah phooey." The Chinese gentlemen threw in their cards. The interpreter said, "Hey, great going, mister, your thousand-dollar bet just won."

Leroy was a lottery player. One day he hit the big jackpot. He decided he was really going to live it up like the big nabobs. He went on a world tour and then he went on a safari. One of the other members of the safari was a fox-hunting Englishman. He asked Leroy to join in the local hunt when he visited England. Leroy did not want to admit he was not to the manor born, so he read up everything he could find on the subject of fox hunting in England. It is traditional for everyone on a hunt to provide his own hounds. And no females among them. This created a problem for Leroy. He didn't own any hounds, and, besides, getting a dog through quarantine into England is well nigh impossible. He would just have to find at least one dog after he got there. It was fox hunting season, and the only dog Leroy could get was a female. The hunt master reluctantly made an exception in his favor because he was Lord Chattelbag's guest. The hunt took off. Soon a fox was sighted and the dogs were let loose. Within minutes the dogs were out of sight. The hunters could hear them all over the woods, but they couldn't find them. The hunt master hailed a farmer walking across a field, "Did you see any hounds go by?" "Yes." "Which way did they go?" "I'm sorry, but I didn't notice. I was so startled at seeing the fox run fifth."

Gamblers are superstitious, as we all know. This horse-player went to the track one day and told all his friends, "Boy, today I'm hot." A few hours later he met a friend who asked, "How'd you do?" "Well, every night for the past two weeks, I've been dreaming about the number six. Today I bet the sixth horse in the sixth race." "What happened?" "He came in sixth."

An enormous car-carrier truck was barreling along the highway one night when suddenly its headlights gave out. The driver couldn't fix them, but he had a very clever idea. He climbed up into the first car on the trailer and turned on its headlights. Then he got back into his cab and started driving again. In the distance he saw a car coming toward him. Suddenly it swerved off the road, crashed through a fence, and landed on its back in a corn field. He stopped his rig and ran over to help. The two men in the wrecked car were badly shaken but not hurt.

"What the heck happened?" the truck driver asked. "Why did you drive off the road like that?"

"We saw those headlights coming toward us," one of the men answered," and I told my friend, Ed, here that if the car coming toward us was as wide as it was high, we'd better got the heck out of the way."

In New York, unemployed actors used to hang around a Times Square drug store to find out what was going on and to get tips for jobs. One day, while Jim and his friend were there, a fellow came in and said, "Are you an actor?" and he pointed to Jim.

"Yeah. I'm an actor."

"Do you want a job?"

Jim said, "Sure, I want a job."

"Come with me."

That night the friends met again.

"Hey, Jim, what's the job? What are you doing?"

"It's a war play, and I'm a sentry. I march up and down as the curtain goes up in the second act. Then another actor comes on as a Captain and he says 'Are you Sergeant Jones?' and I say 'I am.' "

Jim's friend congratulated him. "Gee, that's great. You have a line. That means more money."

Jim said, "Yeah."

Every time the two saw each other, the friend would say to Jim, "Are you Sergeant Jones?"

And Jim would answer, "I am."

Opening night, as the curtain went up for the second act, there was Jim marching up and down in all seriousness. Suddenly the other actor, playing the part of the captain, came out.

"Are you Sergeant Jones?" he asked.

And Jim answered, "Am I?"

6

The Doctor Knows . . .

There was an old fellow of Clure
Whose wife was as thin as a skewer.
Last night, sad to say,
She at last passed away—
Through the bars of a drain down a sewer.

The man had to have a molar extracted, and the dentist was doing a beautiful job. He pulled out the tooth, but suddenly the forceps slipped and the tooth went right down the man's throat. The dentist said, "Don't panic. You'll be all right, but you'd better go to a throat specialist and have him take a look." So he went to the throat specialist and the doctor examined his throat and said, "I don't see anything in your throat. Whatever it might have been has probably gone into your esophagus. I'm going to send you to a chest surgeon." So the fellow, still very anxious, went to a chest surgeon. The chest surgeon looked at him and said, "I can't find anything wrong with your chest. Whatever it was has probably gone into your stomach. I'm going to send you to a gastric specialist." The gastric specialist took an X-ray. He carefully studied the plate and said, "My goodness, I had just discovered that you have a tooth growing in your stomach. You had better go to a dentist."

The prisoner had been going regularly to the prison psychiatrist. One day the psychiatrist said, "Blackie, what an improvement in the last five years! When you first came to me, you hated the sight of me, you had guilt feelings, and you couldn't get along with anybody. Now you're ready to go out into the world, and live a happy and normal life." At that point, Blackie took out a gun, and aimed right at the psychiatrist. "What are you doing, Blackie? I helped you. I cured you." And Blackie said, "Yeah, and now you know too much."

A man walked into a psychiatrist's office and said, "Doc, I need help. I'm obsessed with baseball. Every night I go to bed and I dream that I'm with the Dodgers." The doctor said, "Don't get excited. Tonight when you go to bed, why don't you dream of a beautiful girl?" "What? And miss my turn to bat?"

It had been a terrible accident, and the victim had been lying in the hospital unconscious for three days. Finally he opened his eyes, and the nurse said, "Mr. Jones, you are a very lucky man." "Lucky? Lying here like an Egyptian mummy." "Lucky that you are alive." "Big deal. I'm hungry; could I have something to eat?" The nurse said, "Mr. Jones, we are feeding you right now." "Don't lie to me. Where are the spoons, the forks? I don't see anything." "You don't understand. We are feeding you through a tube. We are feeding you intravenously through your arm." "I'm eating? What am I having?" "We are feeding you borscht." "When you feed me like this, this is nourishing for me?" "It's marvelous for you." "Very good. Pardon me, I'd like to ask you a question. Do you have two more tubes like these?" "What for?" "I would like to have you and the doctor join me for lunch tomorrow."

Frantic the man appealed to the psychiatrist, "Doctor, I can't understand it; you have to help me. Look at my ear. There's a rutabaga growing out of my ear."
The doctor said, "So there is. How did that happen?"
"I don't know. I planted radishes."

This happened in the middle of a cholera epidemic. A

patient looked pleadingly at his doctor, "Doctor, tell me. I can stand it. Tell it to me like it is. What are my chances?" And the doctor looked at the patient and said, "Don't worry about it, old chap. Chances are 100% that you will get well." "You wouldn't lie to me would you, Doc?" The doctor said, "Statistically the prediction stands up. Nine out of every ten people die from cholera. My last nine patients died. You're the tenth. Congratulations."

A lady was eating fish in a restaurant. Suddenly she cried, "Ich, ugh . . . oh, a bone is stuck in my throat. Oh, I'd give a thousand dollars if anybody could get the bone. . . . Ohh." A doctor came over from his table. He said, "Please, don't worry about a thing. Lie back. Don't breathe. Someone please give me a napkin and two forks. . . . There we are." The lady said, "Oh, thank you, doctor. Now what do I owe you?" "Well, why don't you give me half of what you were going to give me before I took the bone out?"

Joe Frisco told a joke once about himself. Joe was in a hospital room and a doctor came in. "Joe, sit here and, when I hit you, cough." The doctor whacked him and Joe coughed. This happened about seven times, with Joe coughing everytime the doctor whacked. Finally, the doctor closed his bag and said, "Joe, how long have you had this cough?"

Worried, the man went to see his doctor. "Doctor, you've got to help me. I wake up in the morning and I feel great. I take a shower, get dressed, go out on the street and suddenly I get spots in front of my eyes and a ringing in my ears." The doctor said, "That is very unusual. Let me examine you." After the examination, the doctor said, "I'm afraid you've got what we call the clarb disease." "The clarb?" "That's it. There is no cure for the clarb disease." The man asked, "How long, Doc?" "Three months at the most." So the man walked out, thinking to himself, "Well, what the heck! I might as well enjoy myself these next three months." He bought a big Cadillac and hand-made shoes and tailor-made suits. He booked for a trip around the world. Then he remembered that he needed shirts, so he went to a shirtmaker and said, "I want twenty-four hand-made monogramed silk shirts." "Yes sir, what size?"

"Thirty-four sleeve, fifteen neck." "Yes, sir, but you know you are a sixteen neck." "I've been wearing a fifteen neck for twenty-two years." "Perhaps you can wear a fifteen neck, but the tightness will give you spots in front of your eyes and ringing in your ears."

A man pleaded with the psychiatrist, "You've got to help me. It's my son."

"What's the matter?"

"He's always eating mud pies. I get up in the morning and there he is in the backyard eating mud pies, and I come home at lunch and he's eating mud pies, I come home at dinner and there he is in the backyard eating mud pies."

The psychiatrist reassured him: "Give the kid a chance. It's all a part of growing up. It'll pass."

"Well, I don't like it, and neither does his wife."

A woman and her husband went to a dentist. She said, "Listen, I want to have a tooth removed, and I want to have it extracted immediately. I don't care about the pain or anything, just pull it right out because we have to get out of here right away. So no novacaine, no sodium pentathol; just pull out the tooth like that." The dentist looked at her and said, "I tell you, ma'am, you are really a courageous woman. I have never met a person like you in my life. Which tooth is it?" She turned to her husband and said, "Show him your tooth."

A real "Casper Milktoast," a real coward, went to a dentist's office. He walked in meekly and said, "I need some teeth pulled but I am a coward. I have no courage at all. I'm afraid." The dentist said, "Don't worry," and he pulled out a bottle of elixer of which the would-be patient took about eight nips. After a few minutes, the dentist looked at him and asked, "Do you feel stronger now? Do you have more courage?" "Have I got courage! Go ahead! I dare you to touch me."

The patient was telling the psychiatrist his troubles, "Besides, Doc, I'm so sleepy that I can hardly keep my eyes open. I'm not getting any rest at all. My wife has a pet goat named Celeste. She insists on keeping it in our bedroom, and it's dreadful. The odor is just unbearable." The doctor said, "Why don't you open the window?" "What? And let my pigeons out?"

A man traveling in Russia developed a violent toothache. He went to Moscow to find a dentist. The dentist examined the tooth and told the man it would have to come out and that it would cost 400 rubles. The man was astounded. "Why does it cost so much to have a tooth pulled? For 400 rubles in American money I could have forty teeth out." "In Russia you can't open your mouth, so we have to pull them out through the ear."

Three friends were standing at the bar one day talking about education. One man said, "I went to Harvard and, because I asked a lot of questions, I became a doctor." Another said, "I went to Yale, asked a lot of questions and became a lawyer." And the third shruged,"I went to Vassar." His two friends protested, "Vassar's a girl's school." "I didn't ask any questions, I just had fun."

A patient in a sanitarium kept walking around and saying, "I'm Napoleon. I'm Napoleon." A nurse went over to him and said, "What did you say your name was?" "Napoleon." "Who gave you that name?" "God gave me that name. God gave me the name of Napoleon." Just then another inmate came along and said, "I never gave him that name."

The man hobbled into the doctor's office and said, "Doc, I'm really worn out. I'm getting old. I just don't have the getup-and-go that I used to have." "Well, what do you expect? You're pushing 65, aren't you?" "I'm not pushing it; I'm dragging it along behind."

The wife couldn't get the oven lit, so her husband stuck his head in the oven and struck a match. There was a "pow" and there he stood with a face full of soot and not one eyebrow. Eventually he had to have a graft job. The doctor used the hair from the hind legs of a cocker spaniel. It was a completely successful operation, except every time the poor fellow passed a fire hydrant, he looked surprised.

A man walked into a psychiatrist's office and the psychiatrist looked up and said, "Oh, good morning, Mr. Bonaparte, how are you?" "I'm not Mr. Bonaparte. I'm Julius Caesar." The psychiatrist said, "I beg your pardon. The last time you were here you told me you were Mr. Bonaparte." "That was by a previous marriage."

One day a man who had been a bookie for many years flipped. The doctors figured he needed a rest so they sent him up to a rest home that specialized in mental cases. Soon he started booking horses there. But since the inmates didn't have any money, they bet with rocks. Someone would put three or four pebbles on the desk, and say, "Ladies Maid in the fourth to win." Or a little later another would come in with his pebbles, and say, "House Maid's Knee in the fifth to place." One man walked in with a huge rock. As he put the big rock down to place his bet, two fellows standing in the corner nudged each other and agreed: "He must know something."

A priest in Brooklyn, Father Bob, worked too hard. His doctor told him, "You need a rest. Go where they don't know you—take off the priest outfit, put on a civilian suit." So Father Bob went to Detroit. While he was there, he went to the Playboy Club. A Playboy Bunny tapped him on the shoulder, "How are you, Father Bob?" "Where do you know me from?" "I'm Sister Teresa. We have the same doctor."

A man had a problem and he went to a psychiatrist. "Doc, you have to help me. I don't know what's the matter, but I have this terrible condition. I can't remember anything. I'm a wonderful salesman, but in the middle of a sales pitch, I forget what I'm talking about. My wife called to tell me to meet her at seven o'clock on Eighth Street. I went to meet her at eight on Seventh. I just can't remember anything." "How long have you had this condition?" "What condition?"

The psychiatrist was walking through the halls of the santarium and as he came down the main corridor he saw a patient up on the ceiling. "What are you doing up there?" "I'm a light bulb." "You come down here." "No, I'm a light bulb." The doctor reached up and unscrewed him, and they started walking down the hall. The porter had been standing there with his mop and looking at them. Now he dropped the mop and started following them. The psychiatrist said, "Get back to your job." "You don't think I'm going to stay there and work in the dark, do you?"

A man went to a psychiatrist. "Doc, you've got to help me. I've gote a big problem." And the doctor said, "Why certainly; just sit down and explain what seems to be the matter." The man sheepishly said, "Well, Doc, I like shoes better than I do boots." The doctor said reassuringly, "Well, there's nothing wrong with that. Many people prefer shoes to boots. In fact, I prefer shoes to boots myself." "You do, Doc? Honest? How do you like them, fried or scrambled?"

The doctor asked the patient, "What seems to be the trouble?" "I have this pain in my head, and it's throbbing and throbbing." "Well, obviously it's from smoking too much." "I don't smoke. I don't even like cigarettes." "How about drinking too much?" "I don't drink. I don't even like liquor." "Well, maybe it's late hours, going out too much . . ." "I'm a bachelor, and every night I'm in bed by 8:30." The doctor thought a moment. "I know what it is; your halo is too tight."

A bum went to a doctor and said, "Doc, I swallowed a silver dollar about five years ago." The doctor said, "You swallowed a silver dollar five years ago? Why didn't you go to a doctor the day you swallowed it?" And the bum said. "To tell you the truth, I didn't need the money until now."

Medical science has finally come up with a cure for a cold. If you have a cold in your head and you don't want it to go into your chest, tie a knot in your neck.

7

The Customer Is Always . . .

A Texas oil millionaire walked into his dentist's office and the dentist asked, "Which tooth is bothering you?"

"Oh, I don't care, drill anywhere. I feel lucky."

A man entered a restaurant and sat down at a table, but he couldn't get waited on. At long last, a waiter came over. The customer, by this time, was in a nasty mood.

"What would you like?" the waiter asked.

"A sardine sandwich."

"Domestic or imported sardines?"

"What's the difference?"

"Domestic sardines cost a dollar. The imported ones cost two dollars."

"Give me the domestic. I'll be damned if I pay their fare over."

A man walked into the most fashionable restaurant in London and, though obviously he had money, he was rather uncouth. He sat down, banged his fist on the table and loudly called for service. Then he picked up a napkin and tucked it under his chin. The maitre d' was horrified. He called a waiter over. "Look at that fellow with the napkin stuck in his shirt. Will you go over and, as tactfully as you can, explain that we don't do that sort of thing in fashionable restaurants."

The waiter went over and murmured, "Good evening, sir. Now what will it be, a haircut or a shave?"

A man went into a New York restaurant. He sat there and sat there, and didn't get waited on. Finally a waiter walked over and said, "It's about closing time, sir; how about paying your check?" "Paying my check? I didn't even get waited on yet." "In that case, there'll only be a cover charge."

A woman went shopping for an Easter outfit and everything that goes with it. Just as she was leaving the store, right near the door, she saw a counterful of pantyhose. The price was such a bargain, she couldn't resist grabbing a couple of pairs, even though she was in such a hurry she didn't really have time to do any selecting. She had to bring them back the next day; they were simply too small. She was sent to the section manager, who asked what was her problem. "It's these pantyhose; I want to return them." "What is the matter? Don't they come up to your expectations?" "They don't even come up to my knees!"

The store was having a sale on sweaters. In the window display was one the man liked very much. That, he decided, was exactly what he wanted to give his wife for a present. He stepped into the store and found himself in the middle of pandemonium. Women were hollering and shouting and ruthlessly shoving each other. He finally managed to grab the sweater he wanted. Then he bulldozed his way through the mob to the cashier, who told him coldly, "You certainly are not acting like a gentleman." "I tried acting like a gentleman, but from now on I'm acting like a lady."

A man walked into a restaurant with his girl friend on his arm. The head waiter said, "You'll have to check your umbrella, sir."

An actor playing a small town in the boondocks was told there was a good place to eat around the corner from the theater. He went to the little beanery, bought

himself a bowl of soup and carried it to a table. Then he
realized he did not have a spoon. He left the soup on the
table and walked back to ask for a spoon. When he came
back the soup was gone. He put the spoon down on the table
and went back to demand another bowl of soup. When he
came back to the table with his soup, he found his spoon
had disappeared. This time he left a note on the table with
the soup: Do not eat or drink this soup. I had my foot
in it." When he returned with a spoon, he found his soup
plate empty and across his note had been written: "So did
I."

A man wanted to buy a suit. As he walked past one
store, he saw a sign: "Our suits last 25 years." He couldn't
believe the claim, so he walked into the place and said,
"I beg your pardon, sir, but is that sign out there correct?" "Yes, it's absolutely correct." "How do you know that
your suits last 25 years?" "Well, I'll tell you. We've been
in business 25 years and nobody has ever come in for a
second suit yet."

A fellow standing outside a hotel stopped a man coming out. "I was thinking of checking into that hotel. I saw
that sign, 'Rooms a dollar and up'—any good?" "Well, I'll
give you a rough idea: I paid a dollar and I was up all
night."

A hippie who was going home for the holidays went to
the airline ticket window to buy a ticket. The ticket cost
$212.10, and all he had was $212.05. Hopefully he shoved
the money to the ticket clerk. The clerk counted it carefully twice.

"You're a nickel short, pal."

"Well, what about it, man? You ain't going to turn me
down just for a nickel are you?"

"Listen, if a hundred people came here every day and
were short only a nickel each, I couldn't afford this job.
No, I won't give you the nickel."

The hippie decided he could panhandle someone for that

nickel. Looking around he spotted a man who could only have been a Texan.

"Hey, man, could you give me a nickel? I want to go home for Christmas."

"Sure, boy, here's a quarter. Take four other bums with you."

The man was very unhappy about his meal and about the service he was getting. When the soup came, it was terrible; it was cold and had lint in it. The salad he had ordered looked like it had been made with boiled lettuce. It was just too much for any man to take. He called the waiter and complained, "Listen, I'm very upset. I've been watching that man over there at the corner table and he's been getting beautiful service and food that looks a heck of a lot more appetizing than mine. I want to talk to the manager about this. Where is he?"

"Sitting over there at that corner table."

The driver of a transcontinental trailer rig went into the diner, sat down and ordered ham and eggs. As he sat there eating, the diner door was slammed open and in strutted a group all wearing black leather Hell's Angels jackets. They converged on the truck driver.

One poked at his ham and eggs, "Hey, baby, how about a little mustard in your coffee? And a little sugar on your eggs?" And he upended the mustard jar into the truck driver's coffee and spooned sugar over his eggs.

The driver said nothing, and just ate his toast.

"How about milk with your water" and the Hell's Angel emptied the milk pitcher into the driver's water glass. Silently the driver took his check over to the cashier, paid his bill and walked out.

The Hell's Angel laughed and turned to the waitress, "Not much of a man, is he?"

The waitress shrugged, gazing out of the window. "And not much of a driver, either. He just ran over seven motorcycles."

A customer walked into a drug store and found a very sexy girl behind the counter. She looked at him and said, "What is your desire?" He looked her up and down and said, "Well, my desire is to jump over the counter and grab you and hug you and kiss you, and make mad passionate love to you. But what I *need* is some mouthwash."

The vacuum-cleaner salesman knocked on the farmhouse door. The lady of the house had barely opened the door when he was inside, talking fast to convince her that the vacuum cleaners he was selling were the best, the fastest, the cleaningest in the whole country. To demonstrate, he pulled out a bag and threw handfuls of dirt on the rug. Every time the lady tried to protest, he would shush her. "Don't worry about a thing. This vacuum cleaner is terrific. If it doesn't pick up every speck of this dirt, I'll eat every bit of it myself." She finally managed to say, "You'd better start eating. We don't have any electricity."

The man was really tearing along when a cop stopped him. The policeman came over, leaned on the door and said, "Do you realize how fast you were going? You were doing 75 miles per hour in a 25-mile zone. Do you realize how many lives you are endangering?" And the driver just sat and listened while the cop kept bawling him out. Finally he couldn't take any more and said, "Wait a minute, officer, are you a servant of the people?" The officer said, "Sure I am." "Well, what are you standing around for? Get me a glass of water."

A woman walked into the pet department of a large store and said to the salesman, "I would like a sweater for my little doggie." The salesman said, "Good. What size does your dog wear?" "Oh, I don't know." "Why don't you bring him in so we can measure him?" The woman said, "Oh, I couldn't do that. I want it to be a surprise."

The television star was a heavy tipper. Stars have to be or people say, "Big star, little tip . . ." He had stayed in this hotel just one night. As he left his room to go down and check out, he saw the maid. So he tipped her a couple of dollars. The elevator operator was obviously keeping one hand open, so the star slipped a buck into it. The clerk behind the desk looked expectant, so he was tossed a buck. Three bellhops each took one piece of baggage—three more tips. Still another bellhop was waiting by the open trunk of the car to lift the baggage in. By this time the television star was getting annoyed. Just then the doorman came over and said, "So long, sir, I hope you won't forget us." The star reached over, took the doorman's hand and said, "Certainly not. I'm going to write every day."

A man sat down at a bar and said, "A martini, please." As soon as the bartender set the martini up, a little monkey hopped up and ran right along the bar and put his paw in the martini. The customer protested: "Hey, what's going on here? I just ordered a martini and that monkey came up and put his paw in it." The bartender said, "It has nothing to do with me. That monkey belongs to the piano player over there. See him about it." The customer walked over and said, "Piano player, do you know that monkey just put his paw in my drink?" The piano player looked up and said, "No, man, but if you've got the sheet music, I'll play it for you."

A couple checked into a motel. "What are your rates?" "Ten dollars a day and up." "Do you take children?" "No, just cash or check."

A man went into a store to buy a suit. He asked the salesman, "What kinds of suits do you have?" "We have only one kind. Its price is $1,500." "What? $1,500 for a suit, that's ridiculous." "Not for this suit. It happens to be the most terrific suit in the whole world. First, we strip you naked and dip you in wax and let it harden. Thus we have a mold of your exact body measurements. In Tibet we have these special sheep. We get all of the wool from them, and this is woven and shipped to Scotland where they do a special dye job. Any color suit you want you can have. A green suit . . . like an elm tree, they will take a tree and squeeze the juice from the leaves for the dye. Anything you want. It is the most fantastic suit. The buttons come from the beaks of African birds. For a suit like that, is $1,500 too high?" The customer was impressed. "Why, that's fantastic. I've got to have that suit. The problem is, I need it tomorrow." The salesman said, "You've got it."

The fussy customer gave the waiter his order: "Give me a cup of coffee, and a ham and egg sandwich on rye toast. I want the toast thin and lightly toasted. I'd like the crust cut off the bread and the caraway seeds picked out. The ham must be very thin and cooked separately from the eggs, and the eggs must be fried in butter. The ham and eggs must be on one slice of toast that has been spread with a little mayonnaise. The other slice of rye toast should have no mayonnaise and be placed on top. You have all that?"

The waiter replied, "Yes, sir. Will you come in tomorrow for a fitting?"

One of the two old sisters had a terrible toothache. She hated going to the dentist. Besides the family dentist had moved to a city it took an overnight bus ride to reach. The pain became unbearable, and she just had to go. Her sister tried to calm her fears. "Here's a pill to relax you. Here are two more—take one when you get on the bus and take the other when you are halfway to the city." As soon as the little old lady boarded the bus, she asked the driver to let her know when they got to Elmira. Every fifteen minutes the little old lady would stagger down the aisle of the bus to ask the driver, "Are we in Elmira yet?" He would answer, "Don't worry, lady. I'll let you know when we are in Elmira." After a while, the driver found the constant questioning annoying. The next time the little old lady came down the aisle he persuaded her that she was bumping into people who were trying to catch a little sleep and that she should stay in her seat and not worry. All of a sudden the driver realized he had forgotten Elmira and the little old lady. Without saying a word, he turned off the thruway onto a road that led back to Elmira, 17 miles away. When they pulled into the bus station, he said to the little old lady, "Here you are. We're in Elmira." "Oh, thank you, but I didn't want to get off here. I promised my sister I would take another pill when I was halfway to the dentist's."

This little old lady stepped nervously into the crowded elevator in a huge skyscraper. The elevator operator pushed some buttons and the elevator shot up toward the fifty-ninth floor. The little old lady was extremely frightened. "Young man," she said to the operator, "if this cable should break, would I go up or down?" He looked at her and said, "Well, lady, it's all according to what kind of life you've lived."

The American tourist's big, beautiful Rolls Royce broke down in the middle of Europe. A mechanic came, looked it over and admitted, "I don't know what to do with it, Mister, but I know someone . . ." So he brought another mechanic and another; soon there were about five or six mechanics around and all baffled. The tourist doesn't know what to do except that he's not going to leave a Rolls Royce in the middle of Europe. Someone suggests they get a man from the next town who is known to tinker with things; so they send for him. Three days later, the man arrived on a mule, got off and looked at the car. "Anyone have a hammer?" "Yes, I do." "Give me the hammer." The man took the hammer and gave one small tap—"Try to start the motor, please." The motor started. "That's fantastic. How much is that?" "One hundred dollars." "A hundred dollars? That's a lot of money for one tap with the hammer." "The tap with the hammer is only one dollar. And $99 dollars for knowing where."

The fellow was strolling along on the lower East Side. As he walked by a clothing store all of a sudden he found himself yanked inside and a salesman was saying, "Well, as long as you're in here, maybe I could sell you a little something?" "As a matter of fact, I do need an overcoat." "I got it for you. There's the overcoat. And in this store we have just one price—$200." "You're talking to a man with one price: I'll give you $50." "To tell you the truth," the salesman answered, "I'm a man with one word—sold."

The contractor was walking around and talking with the lady who had just bought a brand-new house. "I'm here to find out what color you want your rooms painted, ma'am." "This, of course, is the dining room and I'd like to have it beige." "Yes." And with that he walked to the window, opened it and called out, "Green side up, fellows." He followed her into another room and she said, "Now this is the study and I'd like this in nice red." "OK," he said and walked to the window and yelled again, "Green side up, fellows." Together the contractor and the lady went upstairs, and the lady said, "This is the master bedroom and I'd like this yellow." "Yes." Again he opened a window and yelled, "Green side up, fellows." "Now just a minute," the lady protested, "we've been in three different rooms and I've given you three different colors and all you ever say is 'Green side up, fellows'." "You don't have to worry, ma'am, I've got all the colors down, beige, red and yellow. But outside I've got a couple of guys who are sodding a lawn . . . And I have to remind them, Green side up, fellows."

Down on restaurant row, one place was always crowded because it was noted for its fine food. The tips were always dependable and plentiful, so the waiters gradually became lackadaisical and careless. They sort of slid the plates across the tables and tossed down the silverware. One customer became annoyed and he said to the waiter, "I say there, my good man, it is very evident from the manner in which you are serving me that you have never worked at the Beverly Waldorf Hilton Towers." The waiter looked at him and answered, "Yeah, and I can tell from the way you talk to me that you've never eaten there either."

A married couple who had come into a lot of money

decided to educate themselves, and become well mannered and move with the cream of society. They read all the books they could find on etiquette. Then came the day that they went to the most exclusive restaurant in New York. They enjoyed a marvelous meal, beautifully served. When they were through eating, the waiter put in front of them two little bowls with warm water, each with a little piece of lemon in it. The husband said, "What's that?" She said, "I don't know." "Should I ask him?" "Don't show him you're ignorant." He said, "Wait, I'll ask. Waiter, what are these little bowls?" "Their primary function, sir, is that one may wash one's hands in them, should one's hands become sticky during the repast." "Oh." The waiter walked away, and the wife said, "See, ask a silly question and you get a silly answer."

A man was standing at the bar, drinking his beer very quietly. After a while he motioned to the manager standing near the door. The man walked over: "Can I help you?" The customer at the bar said, "You mind if I ask you a question? How many barrels of beer do you sell here a week?" "Well, I think we average about forty barrels a week. Why?" "How would you like to sell eighty barrels a week?" "I'd love to," said the manager. "How would I do that?" The beer drinker said, "By filling up the glasses."

It was a cold and snowy Christmas Eve in Philadelphia. A tramp went into a little restaurant and found the owner. "Buddy, I haven't eaten for days. I'm down on my luck. Could you give me a couple of bucks, it being Christmas Eve and everything." "If I give you two dollars, I know what you will do. You'll go down the street to a tavern and buy a few drinks and it'll be zippo time. You'll be worse off than you are now. I can't do that to you. But if you'll go sit over there at one of my tables like a man, I'll give you the money. When the waiter comes over, you can pick up the menu with dignity and order something and know that you have the money to pay for it. Remember it's Christmas Eve." The tramp said, "Thank you, sir," and sat down. A few minutes later the tramp let out a loud yell.

The owner ran to the table where the bum sat. "What's the matter?" The bum stood up with dignity and said, "What's the matter? You've got some nerve, charging 90¢ for a ham sandwich."

The man always went to the same restaurant and every single day he'd order a beautiful bowl of borscht. And he never complained. One day he came in and got his usual borscht, but as the waiter walked away, the man said, "Just a minute—come here, there's something wrong with this borscht. Taste it." "Look, you're a wonderful customer, if you don't want it, if it's too cold or something, I'll take . . ." "Sit down and taste the borscht." And with this the waiter took the hint, sat down and pulled the plate over to him, and asked, "Where's the spoon?" "Ah hah!" said the customer.

The phone operator in a small town answered the buzzer signal. "Hello?" A voice said, "Can you give me the correct time please?" "When you hear the tone, the time will be eleven thirty." The next day the phone rang again and she said, "This is the operator." "Can you give me the correct time please?" "When you hear the tone, the time will be eleven thirty." This went on for about six months. The same voice at the same time every day. Finally, one day when the caller asked the time, the operator said, "Every day you ask the same question, and pardon me for being sort of personal, but what's it all about?" "I work down at the saw mill and we set our whistle by your clock." "That's strange, we set our clock by your whistle."

The cop stopped the car and said to the driver, "You were going 85 miles per hour." The driver protested, "No, I wasn't. I wasn't even going 65. I wasn't going 40. I doubt if I was going over 30." The cop gave him a ticket for parking.

Business wasn't good at a restaurant that sold nothing but sandwiches, all kinds of sandwiches. The new proprietor finally thought of the right slogan to put in the window: "Any kind of sandwich you want, we have it. If we don't, we'll give you double your money back." One day, a wise guy read the sign, thought a while and decided he knew how to get double his money back. He walked in and sat down. The proprietor walked over and asked, "What kind of sandwich would you like?" "An elephant sandwich." The owner hid his bafflement and said, "That will take a minute, sir," and walked quickly into the kitchen. He stood there for several minutes, chewing his nails. Finally he walked back to the man at the table: "Sorry, sir, I won't be able to give you an elephant sandwich." "Oh, boy, I got you there! I get double my money back, right? You're out of elephants." "No, we've plenty of elephants; we just ran out of bread."

Three girls went to the corner restaurant for lunch. The waiter came over and the first girl said, "I'd like chicken on white." He said, "What's with chicken all the time? Take the roast beef." She said, "All right, roast beef on white." "White? Have wholewheat." She said, "All right, roast beef on wheat." The waiter turned to the second girl: "What are you having?" "I'd like some hot danish; pop it in the oven." He said, "It's hot when it comes to the table. Hot's not good enough?" "All right, just danish. And a cup of coffee." "Coffee will keep you awake at night. Milk, drink milk." She said, "All right, then, milk." The third girl looked up and smiled at the waiter: "Do you have any suggestions for me?" "Suggestions? Who'd got time for suggestions?"

Three badmen had been found guilty of cattle rustling and they were going to be hung by the cowboys—from a tree right near a canyon with a big river below. They put the rope around the neck of the first badman and swung him out on the branch. The noose slipped and he dropped down to the river and swam away. The same thing happened to the second cow thief. The cowboys put the rope around the neck of the third rustler. He looked at them and said,

"Could I have one last request?" "Of course." "Put the noose around my neck real tight. I can't swim."

A hippie just back from India was going through customs. The inspector said, "All right, open your luggage." "I just got a couple of Hershey bars." "Anything to declare?" "No, baby, it's just great to be back, man, wow." "Any pornographic material?" "No, baby." "Any liquor?" "Uh, uh." "A joint?" "No, baby, nothing." "You're sure you don't have any pornographic photographs?" "Baby, I don't even own a pornograph."

A song dedicated to the waiter who never gets an order right: "Take Back Your Heart, I Ordered Liver."

Every day, McTavish went to the little pub the moment it opened in the morning. He walked in, ordered his drink and shouted, "When McTavish drinks, everybody drinks." But there's never anybody there to join him, so he saved his money. One day, the bartender had a great idea. He called up all his friends. The next morning McTavish walked in, looked around and said, "When McTavish drinks, everybody drinks." The doors opened and seventy-five of the bartender's friends walked in and ordered drinks. Without pausing, McTavish put his hand in his pocket and pulled out a coin, threw it on the bar and said, "When McTavish pays, everybody pays."

A customer walked into a bar and said, "I'm really hung over. I've got to have a shot of whiskey." The bartender gave him the whiskey. "Give me a glass of beer, I can't take this whiskey." He drank the beer and started to walk out, saying, "I'll see you." "Just a minute, you didn't pay me for the beer." "What? I traded the whiskey for the beer." "Yeah, but you didn't pay me for the shot of whiskey." "I didn't drink the whiskey, did I?" The bartender said, "I'm not going to get mad. I should, but I'm not. Here's five dollars, go next door to Jim's Bar, he's my rival, go and play the trick on him." "I can't. I was in there ten minutes ago, and he gave me ten dollars to play the trick on you."

It was a train from Glasgow to Aberdeen, and on it there was this little Scotsman who would run out every time the train stopped, buy a ticket and come back in. The conductor was puzzled. "Why do you keep running out at every station and buying a ticket only to the next stop?"

"Well," the Scotsman said, "The doctor told me I have a very bad heart that might give out at any time."

The hotel bar had three entrances. Through the lobby door staggered a drunk: "Hey, bartender, set 'em up." "Sorry, I can't serve you; you've already had too much to drink." The drunk left. Three minutes later he came in another door: "Bartender, set em up." The bartender said, "No. I never serve anybody as drunk as you are." The man left and a few minutes later he came in through the third door: "Bartender, give me a bourbon." "I'm sorry, no drinks." The drunk peered at him: "OK, but do you work in every bar in town?"

A well-known celebrity walked into a bank. The guard recognized him. "Nice to see you, sir." "Thank you. Where do I cash a check?" "Right over there, sir." As he walked toward the window, a girl squealed with delight to see him. The woman in line ahead of him said, "We love you at my house." He thanked her. When he reached the window, the teller said, "Well, well . . . wow . . . in person! We never miss your program . . . What can I do for you?" "I would like to cash a check." "Oh, certainly, sir. May I see your identification?"

The salesman checked into a hotel. The desk clerk said, "You can have a room but we're a little short-handed; you'll have to make your own bed." The salesman didn't want to go look for another hotel so he said, "OK." The clerk gave him a hammer and some nails.

A lady and her little boy were standing on the railroad platform. She asked the station attendant, "Any trains going north tonight?" "Nope, no trains going north." A little later she came back to ask: "Any trains going south tonight?" "Nope, no trains going south tonight." "Thank you." A little later, "Any trains going west tonight?" "No, no trains west." "Any trains going east tonight?" "No, ma'am, no trains going east tonight." She took her little boy by the hand and said, "Come on, Irving, we can cross the tracks in safety."

8

From the Mouths of . . .

If your life is difficult
And rewards are few,
Remember that the mighty oak
Was a little nut like you.

The little boy walked into the dentist's office.

"Is Doctor Anderson in? My mother sent me; I have to have my tooth fixed."

The nurse said, "No, he's not here now; he's away."

"Oh, would you please tell me when he'll be away again?"

The farm boy was a lonesome sort and he worried about going to school. He was afraid he wouldn't make any friends, so he took his goat with him. The first day of school the boy's father was a bit worried. He figured the teacher would send the boy home with a note saying he couldn't bring the goat to school. But nothing happened. And every day the boy took the goat to school with him. At the end of the year the teacher promoted the goat.

The youngster was five years old, and like all five-year-olds he could eat as though his stomach had no bottom. It was his birthday party, and it was his birthday cake. As he put the fourth piece on his plate, his mother protested, "Now, Greg, please, you had candy and ice cream and soda . . . and three pieces of cake already. You'll burst." The youngster looked at the cake on his plate and said,

"Get out of the way everybody. I'm going to have another piece of cake."

The youngster went into the confessional and sat down: "Bless me, Father, for I have sinned." And he proceeded to go through his confession, and the priest gave him his penance.

The boy was just about to go out when the priest said, "Just a minute, I wonder if you will do me a favor?"

"Sure, anything you want, Father."

And the priest said, "Well, you know, I will be here with confessions just when Notre Dame is playing in one of the biggest games of the season, so I won't be able to hear it. Will you go next door to the television store, watch the game and come back to tell me what's going on?"

The youngster said, "OK, Father," and out he went. About an hour later he walked back into the confessional and said, "Bless me, Father, for I have sinned."

"Wait a minute. You've been gone only about an hour; you couldn't have done much of anything in an hour."

"Neither did Notre Dame, Father."

It was his wife's birthday and as he left for work the husband said to her, "I have bought you a present which I will give you tonight, but besides that I would like you to go out and buy something you really want. Here is $100 for you." That night when he came home from work his wife met him happily at the door and said, "Dear, I bought the most beautiful suit with that money you gave me." "Well, where is it?" "In the bedroom." "Let's go; I'd like to see it." They walked upstairs to the bedroom. Just then, the telephone rang and their six-year-old daughter answered, "You can't talk to my mommy right now. She is in the bedroom with daddy. She's showing him her birthday suit."

A ticket clerk at the railroad station was sitting in his office. As the train pulled out, there was a loud scream outside and he charged out of his little office. One of the regular commuters, bloody and disheveled, staggered past him. "What happened, Mr. Snipchard?" the clerk asked. But the man shook his head and mumbled something incoherently. The clerk turned to a little boy standing on the platform. "What happened?" he asked.

The boy answered: "He tried to catch the train."

"Did he miss it?"

"No, he caught it, but it got away."

He was the kind of boy who would run into the kitchen, take eggs and throw them up into the air, and then laugh with glee when they hit him on the head. "The yolks on me," he'd shout. He was driving his mother crazy. She said, "The way you're carrying on, I'm going to wind up an old woman." He said, "That'd be a great way to spend an evening, Ma." Another time, she said, "I appeal to you as a little boy. . . ." He said, "You don't appeal to me as a mother." The mother finally lost her temper: "Go to your room. You're going to bed. Say your prayers and maybe the good Lord will forgive you." He went to his room. His mother followed him and watched while he undressed and got ready for bed. The boy knelt down by the bed, clasped his hands, bowed his head and whispered, "Our Father who art in Heaven." His mother said, "I can't hear you, Billie." "I wasn't talkin' to you."

A postman was sorting some mail out just before Christmas and he saw an envelope addressed to "Santa Claus, Somewhere near the North Pole. Private and Personal." So he opened and read it. "Hey, listen to this," he called. All the sorters came around. "Dear Santa Claus: My daddy is very poor and I don't have a mommy, and he hasn't been well and he hasn't been able to work. We haven't been able to pay the rent and I don't want any presents this year. What I would like is for you to send $50 so I could give it to daddy for a Christmas present. I love you very much."

The postmen were deeply touched by the boy's letter. They took up a collection. It came to $35, short of the amount the boy asked for but still a tidy contribution. Then they put it into an envelope and added a Christmas card on which they wrote: "Per request of Santa Claus." The envelope was delivered the same day. But two days before Christmas one of the mailman saw a letter addressed to Santa Claus. He recognized the boy's handwriting, opened it and read it aloud:

Dear Santa Claus:

Thank you very much for the money. But next time please deliver it yourself. Don't send it through the post office. You see, they deducted $15 for the service.

The man walking down the street was startled to see a man with a baseball bat chasing a youngster down the street. "Hey," he yelled, "why are you trying to hit that boy over the head with that bat?" The man with the bat stopped and came over to stare at the man who had yelled at him. Finally he said, "I'll tell you why. Because he bothers me." "But what can a kid like that do to bother you?" "All day long he keeps asking me for empty boxes." "So?" "I'm an undertaker."

A mother was scolding her little son: "You're a naughty boy. You are a very, very bad boy. I think it's cruel of you to fight with your little brother. And of all the mean, ugly things to do, you kicked him in his stomach." The little boy said, "It wasn't my fault; he turned around."

This youngster had always gotten rotten marks in school. He had never taken home a good report card. One day he came running into the house: "Mommy, mommy, I got a hundred on my report card." His mother was flabbergasted.

She asked, "A hundred in what?"

"Fifty in spelling and fifty in arithmetic."

The little boy was at that age when there is no end to a child's questions—why, why, why. He kept looking back at the woman standing behind his mother in the supermarket line. Suddenly, he poked a finger at her middle. "Why does that stick out?" "Why, that's my baby." "Is it a boy or a girl?" "I don't know, but I love it anyway." "You do? Then why did you swallow it?"

The trouble-making child had been taken to a psychologist. To test the youngster's comprehension level he asked the child, "How many tails has a cat?" "One." "How many feet does a cat have?" "Four." "How many ears?" The child looked puzzled. "Haven't you ever seen a cat?"

The two little children were playing in the sand at the beach. The boy, who was about four, walked over to the girl, who was about his age, and said, "Hi, want to play with me? My name is Joey." "OK. My name is Priscilla." After they had worked silently on a sand castle for a while, the boy said, "I go to church on Sundays. I'm a Catholic." "So what? I go to church, too, and I'm a Protestant. And I don't want to play in the sand any more. Let's go in the water." The boy said, "I don't have a bathing suit." "Neither do I. So let's just take off our clothes." They did and went paddling in the water. Suddenly she looked at him and said, "I didn't know Catholics were so different from Protestants."

A little boy came home from his very progressive school. He went to his mother and asked, "Hey, Mom, where did I come from?" She made a quick decision and said, "Well, uh, the stork brought you." "Oh, and where did you come from?" "The stork brought me too." "How about grandpa and grandma?" "The stork brought them." The boy looked worried: "You mean to tell me there hasn't been a normal birth in our family for three generations?"

Out in the Arizona desert an Indian boy was practicing sending smoke signals. Suddenly he heard an ear-shattering explosion. This big mushroom-shaped cloud rose over the horizon and hid the sun. The Indian looked up and said, "I wish I'd said that."

A member of the Ladies Bridge Club was extremely proud of her little son, a precocious kid. One day she decided to show off to all the other mothers in the club how much her son knew about science. She said to him, "Darling, tell all the ladies what happens when the steam comes out of the tea kettle. What does that mean, son?" He said, "That means you're going to open another one of Daddy's letters."

The driver of the Cadillac had made a wrong turn and then guessed wrong again, and there he was, lost in the back country. The dirt road was too narrow to turn the car around. Ahead was a stream without a bridge, though the road continued on the other side of the water. As the driver wondered about getting out of his predicament, a farm boy came along. The driver called to him, "Hey, boy, is that water shallow?" "Yep, it's shallow." So the man started to drive through the water. Suddenly, there he was, sitting neck-deep in water. "I thought you said it was shallow!" "Funny," answered the boy, "when our ducks wade into it the water barely reaches up to their feathers."

The boy was about five or six years old and, like all boys of this age, dropped his clothes wherever he happened to take them off. A daily task for his mother was to go around the house and pick up his clothes, hang them up or send them to the cleaners. On one such occasion she found a pair of pants under the bed and before sending them off to the cleaners emptied the pockets of the usual miscellaneous gatherings of a little boy. Except this time she found a neatly folded note. She opened it and read: "Puff, puff, draw, puff, puff." The boy was playing outside at the time. She went to the window and called sternly. "Come into the house this minute." "Gee, Mom, why'd you call me in?" "So, you're learning how to smoke!" "No, I'm not." "No? Then what's this note? 'Puff, puff, draw, puff, puff?' " The boy looked at his mother innocently, "Oh, *that!* I'm learning how to play 'Home, Sweet, Home' on the harmonica."

Her two little boys were always in trouble and their mother just didn't know what to do with them. She said to a neighbor, "They are so naughty and always into mischief, I just don't know what to make of my sons." The neighbor said, "Why don't you take them to see the priest." The mother said, "Why, that's a wonderful idea." She went in and said to the boys, "Johnny, Freddie, I want you to promise me that you will go to confession and talk to the priest, confess all your sins and promise that you will be good boys." The boys promised and went off to the church. When they arrived at the church, Johnny said to his little brother. "You stay here, and I'll go in and I'll do it first and see what it's like." He went into the confessional, and the priest behind the curtain asked in a loud voice, "Where is God?" Absolute silence. The priest leaned forward and said even louder, "Where is God?" No answer. He said, "Johnny, WHERE IS GOD?" Johnny ran out of the booth and out of the church, grabbed his brother and together they ran all the way home and hid in the attic. Freddie, all out of breath, said, "What did we run for?" The older boy replied, "You know what? God's missing and they're blaming us for it."

A lot of little kids sitting around heard a fire siren. They waited, and suddenly a big fire engine went by, making a lot of noise. And there next to the driver was the biggest dalmatian dog they'd ever seen. The kids kept wondering what the dog did. One little boy said, "I think he's there because they use him when they get to the fire to control the crowds." Another little boy said, "No. He's there to help unroll the hose." The third little boy said, "You're both wrong. What they do is they let him off and follow him, and that way they find the fire hydrant."

A little boy was waiting for the bus with his mother. She said to him, "Now remember, Charlie, when you get on the bus I want you to say you are 11. If the driver thinks you're 12, we'll have to pay a fare for you and I only have enough money for one of us." Charlie said,

"I'll remember." They got on the bus and the driver said, "Wait a minute, kid. I want to ask you something. How old are you?" "I'm 11 years old." The driver said, "You look older, when will you be 12?" "As soon as I get off the bus."

When little boys get together they brag about their bravery. One youngster said, "Last night I found a rat, and I grabbed it and whacked it down on the floor and kicked him, and hit him over the head, and jumped on him . . ." Just then a minister walked into the room: ". . . and then God came and took him home."

Seven-year-old Gregory went to his mother one day and said, "Mommy, where did I come from?" She became flustered and said, "Wait until your father comes home. He'll explain everything." When her husband came home, she took him aside and whispered, "Gregory wants to know where he came from." So the father went through the whole thing with Gregory . . . about the birds and the bees and the flowers. When he was all through, he asked his son, "What made you ask?" "Well, the kid sitting next to me in school comes from Seattle and I just wanted to know where I came from."

Little Billy came home one day and kept using a very, very dirty word. His father said, "Billy, if you don't say that word again, I'll give you a quarter." "All right, Daddy." So his father gave him a quarter and he went out to play again. An hour later Billy came back again and said, "Daddy, I've got a word that's worth a dollar."

A kid got on a bus and walked to the rear and sat down without paying his fare. The driver called after him, "Hey, kid, you didn't pay the fare." "I don't have to pay." "Everybody has to pay the fare." "Not me." "Look, kid. I'll put you off if you don't pay the fare." Well, I don't have to." "What's so special about you? Why don't you have to pay?" "Because my name is Crime and Crime doesn't pay."

It was vocabulary improvement time for the class. The teacher asked, "What is latitude?"

One boy stood up to answer. "If I do you a favor and you appreciate it . . . that's latitude."

"No, that's gratitude," the teacher said. "But let's start with a simpler word. What is a miracle?"

"It's a fish," the same boy answered.

"No, that's a mackeral," the teacher said. "Don't you know what a miracle is?"

"No, m'm."

"Well, let's say that you went to the fifth story of a building and you fell out of the window and that you didn't get hurt. What would that be?"

"Lucky."

The teacher tried again. "Let's say that you went back up to the fifth story and again you fell out of the window and you didn't get hurt. What would that be?"

"Uh . . . a coincidence."

Still the teacher wouldn't give up. "Let's say that you went up a third time to the fifth story and you fell out of the window and you're fine, you're not hurt at all. What would that be?"

"By that time," the boy said, "it would be a habit."

The little boy was obviously lost. He kept walking around in the department store, great big tears streaming down his face. A clerk said, "Hey, little boy come here. Where's your mama?" "Will you help me find my mama?" "Do you remember what you mother had on?" "Yes, she had on a checkered dress and she had on a little hat and a pocketbook." "What was the last thing your mother told you before you got lost?" "She told me to stay close to her and to hold on to her skirt." "Well, why didn't you do that and you wouldn't be lost now." "I couldn't reach it."

Grandpa had just returned from a visit to the old country. He was telling his grandson all about the trip: "It was a wonderful, exciting experience, especially coming home on that super new plane." "Oh, tell me about it, grandpa." "Well, there were 350 passengers and there were 14 stewardesses and you didn't know you were in the air. It was a remarkable flight." The grandson said, "Grandpa, I want to tell you something. There is a kid in my class whose dad came home once on one of those planes. It had 400 passengers on board. When they got aloft and lowered the lights, and all those the people walked up and down the aisle, well, somebody was mugged."

9

Home Is Where . . .

Said the toothbrush to the toothpaste
In a moment of delight,
I'm gonna give you a great big squeeze
When we meet on the bridge tonight.

Everyone thought they were a lovely old married couple, but the husband was really a nasty old man who always moaned no matter what nice things his wife did for him. Every morning she'd try to please him with breakfast. He loved eggs. She'd fixed him some scrambled eggs, and he'd take a spoon and fill it with jam and throw it at her, because he wanted poached eggs. If the eggs were poached, he'd want scrambled; and if she scrambled them, he'd want poached. The poor old darling was a nervous wreck. She said to her friend, "What can I do?" "Listen, take two eggs and poach one, and scramble the other." She did just that. He looked at the poached egg and he looked at the scrambled egg, and she gave him a little smile. He looked at her and said, "You clown, you poached the wrong one."

A circus was having a big auction because it was going out of business. There was one ferocious tiger, a real man-eating beast. This little fellow walked up and said, "I'd like to buy that tiger." His friend protested: "Are you kidding? You want that horrible beast, that man-eating tiger? Why? Are you going into the circus business?" "No, my wife's away on vacation, and I'm lonely."

"Mr. Johnson, my mama wants to know if you can let me have change for a dollar?"

"Sure, son," he said, and opened the cash drawer, and handed out the change.

"Thank you. See you later, Mr. Johnson."

"Wait a minute, where's my dollar?"

"Mama will give it to you Tuesday."

The man had been working as a ticket-taker at the local movie house for many years. Every night when he came home his children asked, "How did it go today?" With a weary sigh, he would shake his head and answer," Don't ask." After many more years of working at the same job, he finally managed to send his children to college, and they all became successful. One day they all got together and said to him: "Father, you've worked for years to put us through college. In hot summers, in cold winters, in rain, you stood there taking tickets as the people went in to enjoy the movies. It was hard work and you never complained. Now we are rich and we're going to give you enough money to retire and take it easy."

And the father looked at them. "Are you kidding? Retire? And quit show business?"

His wife was bursting with pride over the beautiful diamond ring her husband had given her for their fifteenth anniversary. She told her husband, "I can hardly wait for the party tonight. I just know everybody is going to admire my ring." They went to the dinner party and not one person of the more than a dozen there said one word about her ring although she kept waving her hand around at the slightest excuse. Finally she said loudly, "It's kind of hot in here. I think I'll take my ring off."

The plaintiff in the divorce case said he wanted a divorce on grounds of cruelty. Every night, he told the judge, he came home and there was a derby in the hallway. The judge said, "Wait a minute, are you sure you want a divorce for cruelty?" "Yes, I want it for cruelty. If there's one thing I can't stand it's a woman who wears a derby."

Alice did not have a very good reputation as a driver, though she thought she was one because she could always back out of the garage with her eyes closed. One evening she went out with the car, and her husband stayed home to watch television. Suddenly he heard this horrendous, thundering crash, and there was Alice in the living room, sitting in the car. "Alice, I can't believe it!! How did you drive the car into the living room?" "It was easy—I just turned left when I got to the bedroom."

Two drunks were talking in a bar. One said, "I don't want to go home. I've got the ugliest wife in the world." "You're wrong, buddy. I have the ugliest wife in the world." "I bet you twenty bucks that my wife is uglier." "I'll give you odds two to one. I'll bet forty dollars to your twenty that my wife is uglier." They went to the first drunk's home, and he called out, "Alice, come here." The second drunk looked at her and said to his friend, "I take back what I said in the bar. She is disgusting." "Well, then, give me the forty dollars." "Hold it—you haven't seen my wife yet." They walked to the second drunk's home but they didn't go in. They went around the house and stopped by a wooden trapdoor in the garden. The second drunk pounded on it. "Come up here." A voice said, "Do you want me to put the sack over my head." "No, I don't want to make love. I want you to meet somebody."

A song I dedicated to the father of the new baby: "There'll Be Some Changes Made."

This lovely couple had been happily married for twenty-five years. Their friends all marveled at the fact that they never argued and never fought. One friend said, "It's such a lovely thing to walk into your house. You've been married twenty-five years, and you and your wife still sit there holding hands." The fellow shrugged. "If we ever let go, we'd kill each other."

At a party, this man had had few cocktails, and he was dancing and carrying on. When he and his wife left the party and were going home in their car, his wife said, "Did anyone ever tell you how fascinating, how charming, how truly handsome you are?" He said, "No, no one ever did." "Then where'd you ever get the idea that you are?"

Wives have more trouble with banks than anybody else. They think a checkbook is something else. My wife came in one day and said, "Well, I got my bank account all straightened out, and everything is just fine." "So how come I got a letter from the bank, saying that you are three checks overdrawn?" "That's ridiculous. I took care of that." "Oh no, you didn't. Three checks are going to bounce. You don't have enough money in your checking account." "But I told you I took care of it." "What did you do?" "I just wrote out another check to cover the first three."

The doctor loved to gamble. He had a direct phone line to racetracks to place bets. A compulsive gambler, he used to say to the nurse, "Will this patient live or die? I bet you five to one . . ." The thing he loved most of all was poker. His wife said, "I'm going to leave you if you play poker on Friday night." So he stopped because he loved his wife. Their wedding anniversary fell on a Friday, and he was so nervous, he just had to play poker. The telephone rang: "Hi. This is Bob from the Dispensary. I've got Dr. Brodsky here, and Dr. Sales, Dr. Kane and Dr. Kildare. We need one more to make up a poker game." He said, "I'll be there right away," and hung up. "I've got to go out dear." "On our wedding anniversary? Do you have to go?" "Yes, it sounds pretty serious, there are four other doctors there."

The man and his wife had never had any children but they had a dog they were crazy about. And every morning at eight o'clock the man got up and took the dog for a walk, every morning for seventeen years. And then old dog died. The next morning at quarter to eight the man woke up, and realized the dog was dead. He nudged his wife and said, "Honey, want to take a walk?"

A man came home and said to his wife, "Boy, have I got great news! I have saved enough money for us to go to Europe on a vacation." "That's wonderful, I'm going to go pack right now." "Wait a minute, I haven't saved enough for us to come back."

The poor man came running home one day and said to his wife, "I've just been to a rich man's house and I found him eating crepe suzettes, beautiful crepe suzettes. I've never tasted crepe suzettes in my whole life. Before I die, I'd like to taste crepe suzettes." His wife said, "Herman, I'd like to make you crepe suzettes, but I haven't any eggs." The fellow said, "So you make them without the eggs." She said, "But I haven't got cream." "Make them without the cream." She said, "I don't have sugar." He said, "So you'll make them without the sugar." She said, "You need brandy." "Forget the brandy; we'll do without the brandy." Determined to please him, she made his crepe suzettes. She put them in front of him. He dug in and tasted them. She said, "Herman, how are they?" "You know, if I live to be a hundred, I'll never understand what these rich people see in crepe suzettes."

Two old friends were talking in a bar. One said to the other, "I notice you've always got a lot of money in your pocket these days. It's not like the old days when you used to be broke. You must have found a lucky charm or something." "Yeah, I always keep a lucky rabbit's foot in my money pocket." "A rabbit's foot in your money pocket changed your luck?" "Yeah, one night my wife was going through my money pocket and she touched the rabbit's foot. She thought it was a mouse and she never went through that pocket again."

An absent-minded professor was sitting at breakfast one morning, just drinking his coffee happily, when his wife leaned over and said, "Do you know what today is, darling?" He hesitated a moment and then said, "Why, of course I do, dear. You didn't think I'd forget, did you? Here's fifty dollars; I want you to go out and buy a beautiful dress, and tonight we'll go to that brand-new restaurant you were talking about and afterward we will go dancing." She said, "Oh, thank you." They went to the restaurant and they went dancing, and when they were driving home, she snuggled her head on his shoulder. He said, "Well, was today everything you hoped for, my love?" "Even better. It's been the best Ground Hog Day I ever spent."

Two fellows were on the beach just gabbing and one turned around and said, "Aw, Sophia Loren, big deal. Everybody is talking about Sophia Loren. Take away her figure, her eyes, her hair, her lips, and what have you got?" The other fellow said, "My wife."

The old man was being interviewed by an admiring reporter. "Sir, what exactly is your age, if you don't mind my asking." "I'll tell you. I'll be 97 years old tomorrow." "That's wonderful. You appear to be in marvelous condition." The old man beamed. "Oh, yes, I'm doing fine. And, you know, I don't have an enemy in the world." "Well, that's a beautiful thought, but how do you explain it?" "I've outlived every dang one of them."

The gentleman sitting at the end of the bar was very, very upset. It was obvious enough so that the man on the next stool turned to him and said, "Pardon me, sir, but you seem more than a bit worried about something. Can I be of help?" "I don't know if you can. I recently married a very lovely French girl. Tonight I went to a party, had a few too many drinks, forgot the time, and now it's so late I'm afraid to go home." "Oh, don't worry about that. There's an easy way to find out if it is safe to go in. You go home, take off your hat, open the door just enough to throw your hat in. If it isn't thrown right out again, it's all right to go in." "It sounds like a good idea; but my wife is French, so maybe it won't work." "What have you got to lose?" "OK, I'll do it." In half an hour the worried husband was back, more dejected than before. His bar friend asked, "What happened?" "I threw my hat in just as you suggested and . . ." "And it came flying out?" "Nope. Some other man's hat did."

The woman was sitting in the kitchen with a neighbor. She asked, "Where's your husband?" "I sent him out about three hours ago to buy some groceries for dinner, but George is so absent-minded, it's terrible. If his head wasn't screwed on, he wouldn't know where to put his hat. Three hours he's gone and I bet he's forgotten what to buy." Just then George ran in. "Honey, you won't believe it! But while I was in the supermarket, I met old Mr. Wilson, you know, the millionaire. I took him for a cup of coffee and, by the time we finished desert, I'd sold him an order for a half a million dollars." She said, "You see, he forgot the groceries."

A married couple, trying to live up to a snobbish lifestyle, went to a party. The conversation turned to Mozart: "Absolutely brilliant . . . lovely . . . oh, a fine fellow . . . a genius, Mozart."

The woman, wanting to join in the general conversation, remarked casually, "Ah. Mozart. You're so right. I love him. Only this morning I saw him getting on the No. 5 bus going to Coney Island."

There was a sudden hush and everyone looked at her. Her husband was shattered. He pulled her away. "We're leaving right now. Get your coat and come." In the car, as they drove home, he kept muttering to himself. Finally, his wife turned to him.

"You are angry about something."

"Oh, really? You noticed it?" he sneered. "My god! I've never been so embarrassed in my life. *You* saw Mozart take the No. 5 bus to Coney Island! You idiot! Don't you know that the No. 5 bus doesn't go to Coney Island?"

An inveterate poker player went out one night and soon found a good game going. He hit a real winning streak. One o'clock, two o'clock, three o'clock—he just couldn't quit because he was still winning. The game finally broke up at five in the morning. On the way home he kept wondering how he would be able to square things with his wife. Suddenly, he stepped into a phone booth and called home: "Don't pay the ransom. I am on my way home."

The man and his wife decided to take a boat trip to Mexico about a year ago. She was the kind of tourist who insists on bringing bags and bags of clothes. They were down at the pier, checking this box and that bag and this suitcase to see that nothing had been forgotten. Suddenly he said to her, "Sweetheart, I wish we had brought the piano." "Don't be so sarcastic." "Honey, I'm not being sarcastic. I left our tickets on the piano."

A lady owned one of those little general stores. Her husband had passed away, but fortunately his insurance policy left enough to cover the mortgage and she was able to eke out a living with the store. Everything went quite well except she had a tremendous problem with mice. She bought a beautiful cat that had been trained to catch mice. After that she got along fine until a darn Yankee driving through one day, very fast, ran over the cat. He was really upset and the sheriff said, "What are you going to do about Miss Johnson's cat?" So the fellow picked up the cat and went into the store and said, "Madam, I was coming down the highway and I . . . I . . . I ran over your cat. I'm very sorry about it, and I want you to know that I come to you in all honesty and I will do anything I . . . . Can I replace your cat?" She said, "Well, that sounds fine to me. How many mice a day to you think you can catch?"

Theme song for some wives/husbands: "Let Me Call You Sweetheart, I've Called You Everything Else."

The house was decorated with beautiful antique furniture. A guest was horrified to see her hostess' seven-year-old pounding nails into an authentic Louis XIV table and the hostess sitting and seeing it without saying a word to stop it. Finally, guest or not, she couldn't keep still any longer. "Isn't that an expensive way to learn how to use a hammer?" The mother replied, "It's not too bad; we get the nails wholesale."

He had been driving for forty or fifty years, and his wife was the worst back-seat driver in the world. The moment he turned on the ignition, she started squawking. She was driving him out of his mind. He finally decided to buy a motorcycle with a side car. He figured that its noise would cut down on her noise. One day he was driving along the freeway and she was in the side car screaming, "Do this, do that." He kept driving along, until a cop pulled him over. "Excuse me, buddy, but do you know that you lost your passenger about two miles back?" "Oh thank goodness I thought I was going deaf."

All that parents talk about today is kids, kids, kids and all the problems and troubles with them. These two fathers were talking and one said to the other, "Do you have a generation gap in your family?" "I don't know, we don't talk to each other."

The little old lady was very hard of hearing. The other residents around the Army base always jumped when those big old cannon were fired off at sundown. She just straightened her dress, patted her hair, looked expectantly at the door, and said, "Come in."

The new dog owner asked a friend of his to come see the new dog that he had just bought for his wife. When the friend came, the man met him at the door. "Go on in;

I'll be right with you." All of a sudden a huge dog ran into the livingroom barking and growling and jumped on the visitor. Frightened, he yelled, "Help me! Call off the dog!" The owner reassured him, "Don't worry! He's really friendly." "Friendly? He's going to bite me!" "Oh, no, he isn't. Remember the old proverb: A barking dog never bites." "I know that proverb and you know that proverb, but does the dog?"

A typical stage mother was always exploiting her daughter who, the mother thought, had a beautiful singing voice. All the theatrical agents in town knew the woman and shied away from her. One day a young agent came into town. The mother grabbed him, sat him down and said, "Oh, my boy, you've got to listen to my daughter. She's got the most wonderful voice." So the agent said, "All right, I'll listen." So the woman put on a record. "Listen, if she doesn't sound just like Lily Pons . . . she's wonderful." The agent listened for a while and then declared, "Say, that IS Lily Pons, singing." "See, she sings just like my daughter."

The couple had gone to see a marriage counselor. Each accused the other of starting their continual arguments. The counselor listened to their squabbling for a while and then said, "You can't both talk at once, so why don't you"— he turned to the husband—"tell me your side first. You'll probably find out you are quarreling about nothing." The husband answered, "Nothing, huh? Well, the other day she threw my suit down the stairs." The counselor said, "Maybe she dropped it. That's nothing to fight over." "Nothing, huh? I was in it."

Sam was a very good husband and provider and a very generous man. He bought his wife all kinds of gifts. But being a practical man, he'd buy her a pair of shoes for her birthday, or a girdle or a coat. Something she could use. One day they came into a lot of money. Hinting that he could now afford to buy her a mink coat got her nowhere, so she took him to the furriers and showed him the coat she wanted. But, practical man that he was, he refused to take the hint. For her birthday that year he bought her a beautiful cemetery plot. The following year, she hinted again about the mink coat. "Honey, why don't you buy me a mink coat this year?" "Are you kidding? You didn't even use last year's present."

One man divorced his wife and then married her sister. He didn't want to break in a new mother-in-law.

The poor woman was married to a real sot. He spent all his time drinking, and his money as well. In desperation she finally appealed to the priest for advice. The priest said to her, "The only way to get your husband to stop drinking is to put the fear of God into him. I happen to know his favorite bar. There's a graveyard on the way home from there. You hide there and wait for him to go by. As soon as you see your chance frighten him." The wife went to the cemetery, draped a white sheet over her and waited behind a tombstone for her husband to come walking by. Long after midnight he came staggering by. The woman jumped up flapping the sheet and shrieking. Her husband peered at the apparition and said thickly, "Shcuse me, I don't believe I've had the pleashure of meeting you." His wife shrieked from under the sheet, "Don't you know who I am?" "No, I shure don't." "I am the devil." "No kidding. We're related to easch other. I'm married to yer shishter."

The husband went to a marriage counselor. "I'm having trouble with my wife." "Yes?" "We're uptight about everything. We're not getting along at all." The counselor advised him, "For a good marriage you have to have a great time. Get out and do things together. And really enjoy yourselves." "OK, I'll try it." The husband went home and, as he walked in, called to his wife, "Hey, honey, how about going out tonight and having some fun?" "Fine. And if you get home before I do, leave the light on."

Anyone who lives 100 years is news, and the reporters

were there at the party for the gentleman's hundredth birthday. "Sir, would you tell us the secret of your longevity?" "Well, I guess it could be a lot of things, but I guess mainly, of course, toadstools." "Toadstools?" "Yup, never ate 'em."

The little boy's father said to his son, "I want you to go down the street and get some cigarettes for me." The little boy went into the kitchen like a good little boy and said to his mother, "I have to get some cigarettes for Daddy from the store." She said, "You can't go, Michael." "But Daddy wants . . ." "You cannot go. That freeway has been built and there's an entrance right where you'd have to cross and the traffic never stops. You can't cross the street; you'll be killed. Let your father go."

A man was walking through the zoo, looking at all the animals. Finally he came to an animal he didn't recognize. It was a baby deer. He walked over to the attendant and asked, "Pardon me, but can you tell me what kind of an animal that is?"

The attendant laughed. "You're kidding! You don't know what that animal is?"

"I'm afriad not."

"Well, what does your wife call you every morning?"

"How do you like that!" The man looked at the animal in amazement. "That's a jackass?"

Mike was a man with a drinking problem. His wife was constantly nagging at him to stop drinking. One night they went together to the company Christmas party. There was plenty of liquor available, and Mike soon had had more than his wife thought he should. She kept saying, "Mike, come on, let's go home." Just as she was about to get him out the door someone proposed a toast to the boss. Mike said, "We can't go now. I can't turn down a toast to the boss." Someone shoved a glass into his wife's hand and she had to join in the toast. She took a small swallow and said, "Ugh, that's horrible-tasting stuff!" Mike said, "You see—

and all the time you've been thinking I've been having a good time."

When you've made good, you naturally want to do something nice for your parents and relatives. The successful lawyer wanted to get something extraordinarily nice and expensive for his mother's birthday. She wouldn't move out of the ghetto she lived in because it was the only life she knew. What could he give her? He finally decided on a beautiful parrot. A brilliant bird, it spoke seven languages —German, French, Arabic, Chinese, Japanese, Hebrew, Italian. He paid cash for the bird and had it shipped to her apartment. The next day he couldn't wait to go to see her; he wanted to see the expression on her face. He walked in and said, "Momma, how'd you like it, the bird?" She said, "Sweetheart, it was delicious." He said, "Ma, you didn't cook that bird? That bird spoke seven languages! How could you cook it?" She said, "So, why didn't he say something?"

Dolores Doright, a good Catholic, was having trouble with her husband, Dudley. Dudley was always drunk. Dolores had tried everything including Alcoholics Anonymous. Finally she appealed to her priest: "Can't you do something about him?" The priest promised: "Bring him in and I'll talk to him." So she brought Dudley in, and the priest talked to him for an hour and Dudley just kept on drinking the whole time. Finally the priest said, "Now listen, Dudley, I have just about exhausted my patience. If I see you drunk one more time, I'm going to have to excommunicate you." The very next day, the priest was out walking around and met Dudley, drunk again. Dudley looked up and said, "Out of the way, Father, and let a good Protestant pass."

A man walked into a sporting goods store and said to the clerk, "Give me forty-four rounds of ammo; and I'd like a pistol, an M-1 carbine and a big Bowie knife." The clerk said, "Yes, sir" and wrapped it all up. "Gee, I hope you have a nice vacation. Where are you going?" "I'm going to visit my son at college."

Theme song for newlyweds: "My Heart Belongs to Daddy, and Everything Else Belongs to the Finance Company."

A very rich couple decided, because their children were all grown up and out in the world on their own, that they should adopt an elderly refugee couple. They had made all arrangements and on the special day went down to the pier and watched the ship come in from Europe. Streams of people got off. Mr. and Mrs. Richdough gradually became more and more nervous.

"What if they don't like us? Or America?" Mrs. Richdough said. "What if they decide to just turn around and go back to Europe?"

"Don't worry, dear. We won't give them a chance to have any regrets. They're going to be too busy enjoying themselves to say anything."

Finally Mrs. Richdough saw a sweet little old lady come down the gangplank. "Look at that darling little old lady. She reminds me of my grandmother."

Her husband said, "And right behind her is a marvelous old man! He must be 85 years old, at least. And he's spry and smiling. He reminds me of my grandfather. That's them! That's the couple we're going to adopt."

They rushed over to the little old lady and the old gentleman and said, "Come with us."

The little old lady started to protest but Mrs. Richdough shushed her. "Surprise! Surprise! Welcome to your new country."

As they put the newcomers into their limousine, the little old lady said, "I would just like to get. . . ."

"We'll take care of everything. Your baggage will be brought to the house and if you need anything, we'll have it delivered."

"But . . ."

"Please . . . there will be plenty of time to thank us later on. Right now you must enjoy yourselves!"

The limousine brought them to the house. There a magnificient dinner had been prepared. The little old lady and the old gentleman ate and drank. Afterwards there were guests to meet them, music, a party. Later when everyone had gone, the little old lady turned to Mrs. Richdough.

"You don't know how much I enjoyed myself. But I must—"

"Not a word," Mrs. Richdough insisted. "I know how tired you are. Tomorrow we can talk and you can thank us. Now you must go to bed." She led the elderly couple upstairs to the master bedroom, and quickly shut the door.

The next morning when everyone came down to breakfast, Mrs. Richdough said, "I know that yesterday we didn't give you a chance to tell us how you felt, but now you can tell us what you wanted to say."

The little old lady said "I do want to say thank you for all the nice things you have done. But there's something I would like to know."

"Of course. What is it?"

"Who's that little old man you've got rooming with me?"

10

Business Is Business . . .

Say it with flowers, say it with eats,
Say it with kisses, say it with sweets,
Say it with jewelry, say it with drink,
But always be careful not to say it with ink.

An applicant for a position in an elegant department store was interviewed for the job. "Where have you been the last few years?" "Yale." The personnel manager asked no further; he hired the man immediately, thinking to himself: Yale, wow! The new employee was put in charge of money and ordering.

One day not much later the personnel manager saw him jamming shut a valise loaded with money and heading fast for the door. With a flying tackle the manager nabbed him. "I caught you—you're the guy from Yale, but I can't remember you name."

"Yim Yackson."

Two bankers were talking and one said, "You know we have a lot of men depositors but we don't have many women depositors. We've got to start a campaign to get more women depositors into the bank."

The other banker said, "You'll never be able to do that. They hide their money either in their stockings or in their bra."

"Well, can't we tell them to put it in the bank where it's safer?"

"Nope, they'd much rather put it where it draws the most interest."

The man was bankrupt. When he came home, he was almost afraid to look at the mail. He picked up one letter and read: "Dear Sir: We are surprised that we haven't received anything from you." So he sat down and wrote back: "There's no reason for surprise. I didn't send anything."

A peddler went through the streets, calling out, "Needles, pins, buttons . . ." A window opened, and an old lady looked out. "Mr. Peddler, would you come up with your wares?" "All right." "Mr. Peddler, I wonder if I could have a package of needles?" So he sold her the needles and she gave him a quarter. "Goodbye, ma'am." She said, "I hate to ask you this, but you know, I'm an old maid and I've never been married, and I'm getting on in life, and I wonder if I couldn't ask you to give me a little hug?" The peddler said, "Oh, no, heaven forbid. I am a married man. I couldn't hug you. What would my wife say?" "I wouldn't say a word to anyone." So he went over and put his arms around her and gave her a hug. "So there, you have been hugged—good day." He had just made it to the door when she said, "Peddler, could I have one more little thing? I wonder if you would be so kind as to give me a little kiss?" "I knew one thing would lead to another. No, I couldn't. I've never fancied any lady other than my wife." "Don't you want to make a little old lady very happy?" He said, "Oh, very well then." And he gave her a kiss. And she pressed something into his hand and said, "Thank you very much." And he walked out. He opened his hand, and there was a five dollar bill. And he walked on down the street saying, "Needles, pins, buttons, kisses."

A salesman had been out on the road for a week. He decided he ought to send his boss at the office a telegram: "Dear Jules, I'll be back day after tomorrow. Everything is fine. Reorders have been terrific. Signed, Hobart."

The telegraph clerk said, "That will be $1.70." "That's too much just to let my boss know I'm coming home." The telegraph clerk said the charge was ten cents a word, so why couldn't he cut out a few words? "That's a good idea. I don't have to say 'Dear Jules' because he certainly knows his own name. If everything wasn't fine, would I be coming back yet? Likewise with the reorders. If I hadn't made my quota, would I be coming home? Do I have to say 'Signed'?" "No." "So what does that leave?" "Just your name, 'Hobart'." "Good. Send it collect."

A little man used to come into a little restaurant in New York every day and order a steak. He'd cut off the tip of the steak and put it in a plastic bag. Then he would eat the rest of the steak and leave. A waiter had watched this year in and year out. One day he walked over and said, "Sir, please excuse me, but I've been with this restaurant for twenty-two years and you've been coming in here every day for twenty-two years. I'm leaving today, and I must know why you cut the tip off your steak." "It's none of your business of course, but since you are leaving, I am going to tell you. That gentleman over there in the green suit is my partner, and he hasn't spoken to me for twenty-two years. I come in and he knows I order steak every day, and he's sitting there hoping I'll choke on the first bite."

An ugly rumor in town started a run on the bank. All the depositors lined up outside waiting for the bank to open. Along came a little woman with a kerchief on her head, and she kept pushing her way to the front. Since she was rather elderly, people allowed her to move through the line. Gradually she excused herself all the way to the front door. She said to the guard, "Excuse me; open the door, please." He said, "What's your hurry? Do you have a lot of money in the bank?" And she looked at him, and said, "Money? Who's got money? I'm waiting for a calendar."

Just as an Indian was trying to check into a hotel, another Indian showed up. The clerk said, "All our rooms are filled. There's a big convention in town." So the first Indian and then the other pulled out a big roll of bills, and the clerk started thinking of a big tip. "I do have one room. It has only one small bed, but I think you'll appreciate the feather bed." The Indians agreed to take the room together. They went upstairs. The room was tiny and the bed was the worst they had ever seen—solid brick. The two of them finally managed to fall asleep. About 2 o'clock in the morning one Indian nudged the other, "Hey, why don't we change places? Your turn to sleep on the feather."

It was a very exclusive, posh hotel—the Dorchester in London. A bellhop was going through the corridors whistling. The manager came along and heard him. "We don't whistle in the corridors of this hotel." The bellhop said, "I'm not whistling, sir; I'm paging someone's dog."

A man walking along the street saw a cat drinking out of a saucer by a little grocery store doorway. He happened to be an art connoisseur and something caught his eye. He went back for a second look and said to himself, "My goodness! That little pussycat is drinking out of the lid of a Ming vase. It must be worth thousands."

He stepped into the store quickly and said to the man behind the counter, "Hi, I was walking by and saw your little pussycat out there."

"You saw him drinking milk, didn't you?"

"Yes, and he's such a skinny little thing, I thought I'd give you five dollars for him."

The storekeeper shook his head. "No, sir."

"Twenty?"

Again the man behind the counter refused.

"Twenty-five?"

"All right. The kitten is yours." He took the money and rang it up on his cash register.

"By the way, the kitten was drinking out of an old saucer. Why don't you just throw that in with the deal?"

"Not a chance, man. That happens to be my lucky saucer. So far this week, I've sold fourteen cats drinking out of it."

The wealthy old Italian had a beautiful home. One day, a visiting relative said to him, "How did you acquire this wealth?" He said, "When I came from the old country I was a poor boy. It was murder. I had no place to sleep and no clothes. I was starving. One day I decided that I wasn't going to starve, so I built a pushcart. I stocked it with all kinds of fruits and vegetables. I walked in the streets and sold the fruit. The next day I sold more fruit. Then I got two pushcarts. Soon I sold more and got five pushcarts. I added potatoes and rutabagas. Then I got three trucks. Then I got five trucks and pushcarts. I'm selling food and more food. . . ." "So that's how you made your money?" "No, last year my aunt died and left me two million dollars."

The Indian was having trouble with his taxes and an agent from the Internal Revenue Service was helping him fill out the forms. "How old are you?" "Ugh." "How many dependents do you have?" "Ugh." "How much did you earn last year?" "Ugh." "Are you self-employed or do you work for somebody else?" "Ugh." "You must tell me these things, because if you tell me everything and I get it all written down here, the government may pay you a refund." The Indian said, "Oh, really, how much?"

He was probably the world's worst boxer, but somehow his manager got him a fight with the champion. Without even trying, the champ was beating him to a pulp. There wasn't a spot on his body that wasn't welted black and blue. At the end of the second round, as the manager rubbed him down in his corner, he said, "I'm not doing so good out there, am I?" The manager patted the boxer's shoulder and said, "Don't worry about a thing. On the radio you are winning. The announcer is a friend of mine."

A fellow was being interviewed down in Texas. He was a very rich man, and the reporter was asking him how he made all of his money. "Well," he said, "I was kind of a poor fellow when I got here. My wife and I had a small sheep ranch. We had several head. And one day my wife was dyeing a bedspread with some blue dye and one of the sheep accidentally fell into the dye. And I had a little blue lamb there. Cute, but I figured I'd have to get rid of it but a tourist came along and said, "I'll give you fifty dollars for that lamb." That gave me an idea: I started dipping all the little lambs different colors. And we sold them like crazy. We'd get 100 to 200 dollars for these lambs. And that's how I made my fortune. I became the biggest lamb dyer in Amarillo."

The dog in the pet-shop window was just the kind he wanted, so he walked into the store and asked, "Is that dog in the window a good one? Does he have a good pedigree?" "What do you mean—good pedigree?" "Does it have a family tree?" "He doesn't even have a flower pot."

At the salesmen's meeting of the dog food company, the president of the company addressed the staff. "I want to say that I am proud of being the president of the finest company in the dog food business. This year alone we have spent a million putting up a new, hygienic, automated factory to produce tasty food for the dogs of this nation. We also have a tremendous advertising budget, and I am proud of our aggressive sales force. Yet, for the first time in years, sales have dropped to an all-time low. I'd like to hear your explanations. Mr. Dowley, as the oldest salesman we have, may we hear from you first." "Well, sir, the answer is simple. It's those blasted dogs—they won't eat the stuff."

Algonquin J. Calhoun was Kingfish's lawyer, and Kingfish had lost the verdict again. Calhoun said, "I will appeal this case to the Court of Appeals." The fellow who had won said, "I'll be there." "My enthusiasm shall not be daunted. I will take this case to the Supreme Court if need be, to the fountainhead of supreme democracy and justice." "I'll be there." "I remain undaunted. I will take this case to the doorstep of Hell." "Well, in that case, you'll have to see my lawyer."

A businessman was in trouble with the tax department. They called him in for an investigation and told him to bring his books along. The investigator went through the books and couldn't make head or tail of all kinds of short-hand notes and mysterious markings, spots, hieroglyphics. Finally he said, "I can't make sense out of all this. I want to know just three things: How much money you took in, how much profit you made, and how much did you draw." The businessman answered, "Are you kidding? These things I wouldn't even tell my own partner."

A hardworking grocer had built up a marvelous business, and everything was going great. One day, as he was delivering groceries in his truck, an old lady stepped out of a lane in front of his truck. He knocked her down and hurt her badly. The court awarded her a tremendous sum for damages —and the grocer was ruined financially. But he was determined to be a success and he held down three jobs, worked hard and built up another grocery business. While he was delivering groceries, his truck skidded and knocked down another old lady. Sure enough, six months later, damages broke him again. But he was never one to give up. This time he got four jobs and saved his money and worked until he again had the best grocery business going. Then another accident, another old lady, court case, more damages, and he was wiped out. This time he sat in his living room and didn't know if he would have the strength to try again. Suddenly the door flew open and his son ran into the room. "Daddy! It's Mommy! Mommy's been run over by a great big truck!" "Oh, thank the lord, our luck's changed at last."

Mrs. Newrich wanted an oil painting of herself to hang over her fireplace. She went to a noted painter and told him exactly what she wanted. The sittings took weeks. Finally one day she said, "I want to see the painting." The artist protested that it wasn't finished yet, but she insisted. She took

one look and screamed, "It's terrible! I look like a monkey!"
The artist said, "You should have thought of that before you
asked me to paint you."

A department store decided to improve its staff, increase
service and efficiency and cut down on costs. They announced
that they were hiring several executives and soon were
flooded with applications. One applicant had a very im-
pressive background as an efficiency expert.

"I want this man," the president of the company said. And
the man was hired. On his first day in the store, the president
called him in to give him instructions. "I want my orders
carried out without question, immediately and to the letter."

"Yes, sir."

"We've been spending too much money. Our employees are
too lax. I want you to walk through the store and check on
all operations. You have the authority to fire anyone on the
spot if you find that the work is inefficient or unnecessary. Pay
them and get them out!"

"Yes, sir." The efficiency expert put his carnation in his
buttonhole and went to work. As he made his rounds, he
noticed a little fellow walking down an aisle with about
three packages in his arms, whistling and stopping casually
here and there to look at the goods on display. After about
five minutes, the little man put the packages down and
stood looking around. The efficiency expert watched him
for a few moments and realized that the man was goofing
off.

"Hey, you, boy! Come here!" he demanded. The little
man shuffled slowly up to him. "How much do you make?"

"I make $75 a week."

"That's money thrown away." He wrote out a voucher
and handed to the man. "Here's a voucher for $75. Take
it over to the cashier at once. When you get the money, get
out of here."

The little man shuffled over to the cashier, cashed the
voucher and left the store. The efficiency expert watched
him leave, then turned to the floor manager.

"How long has *that* man been working here?" he asked.

"He doesn't. He just came in to deliver a couple of packages."

The young fellow wanted to get a job on a boat. He told the captain, "I know all about working on a boat. I was never a sailor but I've read a lot of those sea stories and I know exactly what to do." The captain said, "All right, let's say a tremendous storm comes up starboard. What's the first thing that you'd do?" "I'd throw out an anchor." "What if a big storm came up port?" "I would throw out an anchor." "What if a storm came up aft?" "I would throw out an anchor." "Wait a minute. Where are you getting all the anchors?" "Same place you're getting all the storms."

The man had been called in for an investigation of his tax declaration. The tax man said, "Looking over your form, there's something I don't understand. You've got $500 here for hay." "That's right." The investigator said, "You don't live on a farm and you don't have a horse, yet you claim a $500 expense for hay?" "I just got my pay check and I cashed it and I'm walking over a bridge and somebody yelled, 'Hey' and I dropped the money in the water."

Today you can't get any kind of a job without an education. This poor young man was very ambitious but all he could get was a job as a street cleaner—and he was happy enough to have that. But when his superiors found out that he had no education, and could neither read nor write so much as his name, they fired him. The young man had to make a living, and since he couldn't get another job, he borrowed a few dollars and bought a pushcart. He went around the streets selling whatever goods he could pick up cheaply. Soon he worked out a deal with another pushcart peddlar, selling him some of the goods he had at a small profit. And to make things short, in about three years our hero had pushcarts all over town. Another few years and he had opened big stores, and finally became a millionaire. One day he dropped in his bank to cash a check himself instead of sending his company treasurer to get the money for him. He put an 'X' where his signature was supposed to go and handed the check to the teller. The teller was amazed. He hurried in to the president of the bank and asked, "How can I cash this check?"

And the bank president, too, became flustered. He came out and said, "We know you, of course. Your company has kept its account here for many years. But why did you put an X instead of your signature on the check?"

"I can't read or write."

The bank president looked at him in astonishment. "You're worth millions! You're one of our greatest business geniuses! Just think what you could have done if you had had a good education!"

"If I had an education, I'd still be cleaning streets."

The gate between heaven and hell broke down. St. Peter came out and looked over the situation and called, "Hey, Devil."

"Yeah?"

"According to our agreement, it's your turn to repair the gate."

The Devil said, "I don't have time. All my men are busy and we can't do it."

St. Peter said, "If you don't, I'll sue you."

And the Devil answered, "Is that so? Where are you going to find a lawyer?"

The two were business partners, though one was sort of aggressive and the other was sort of quiet. The quiet one came into the office about 11 o'clock one morning, and the aggressive one said, "Well, how did the meeting go?" "What meeting?" "You idiot! Didn't you go to the meeting at 10:30? You've missed nine meetings in a month. You never remember anything. What's the matter with you?" "I don't know. I remembered the meeting earlier, but on the way here I went shopping and I forgot all about it." "We're going to go bankrupt if you don't do something. Why don't you get a system? Get a notebook and write things down, like 'Max— 10:30 tomorrow, laundry.' 'Max—11 o'clock office meeting,'

'Max—2 o'clock lunch.' Get organized." "Sounds like a great idea." So he got a notebook, and three weeks later he saw his partner again. "It was really a great idea you had—this notebook. My whole life's in order." "Good." "Just one thing I want to know." "What?" "Who is Max?"

Joe and Charlie had been partners in business for years. Then they had a few arguments and split up. One day Charlie got a long distance call from his ex-partner. "Hello, Charlie. You know, I'm one of those who always feel that bygones should be bygones. There should be no problems between us; we should always be friends." "I guess that's right, Joe." "I'm kind of in a spot here. I've got a problem and maybe you can help me out. I need $200 right away." "What did you say?" "I need two hundred dollars right away." "What?" "I need two hundred dollars right away, Charlie." "I can't hear you." The operator cut in and said, "I can hear him." "Then you send him the $200."

This fellow arrived in Heaven and he said, "Lord, I'm here." Then he looked around—and there was St. Peter and there was the Lord and there was an angel playing a harp. He said, "Lord, it's nice up here, but where's everybody?" And the Lord said, "This is it." "Huh? This is it? Is there any way I can look at the other place?" "Certainly," said the Lord, and he parted the clouds. And the fellow looked down and saw the *other place* was jumping and swinging. There was even a twenty-piece band. He said, "Lord, look at them down there swinging! And look at that twenty-piece band! And you've got nothing but a harp." The Lord looked at him and said, "You don't think I'm going to hire a big band for four people, do you?"

Like most panhandlers who make a good living at it, this one had had to become a student of human nature. When he saw a very handsome man walking along the street with the ugliest of women, he fell in step with the man and said, "My, what a beautiful lady you're out with! Could you spare a dime for a cup of coffee?" The man reached for his wallet. "Here's $5.10. The dime is for coffee. For the five bucks, get yourself a pair of glasses."

A producer had had a severe coronary. He had been rushed to the hospital and put in an oxygen tent. He was fighting for his life. A playwright who had tried for months to meet him sneaked into the hospital and up to the producer's room. He waited and waited until the nurse left the room, then he dashed in and lifted the edge of the oxygen tent: "I've written a play, and you've got to read it." Weakly, the producer protested: "Are you crazy? The doctor has given me only an hour to live." "Don't worry—reading this will take only about forty minutes."

The church membership was having a special fund-raising meeting. The minister said, "We haven't any money left in our treasury, and we've got to raise some. We need funds. You, the brother in the front row, aren't you going to contribute something?" And the fellow answered, "I'd like to but I owe everybody in town." The preacher asked, "Don't you think that you owe the Lord something?" "I do. But he isn't pushing me like the other creditors."

Heaven forbid the weather should be anything but perfect on the day of a matinee; if it isn't, attendance will drop. One day it was raining cats and dogs at matinee time. When the curtain went up, one lone old man was sitting in the very center of this theater in Omaha. The star of the play was touched by this loyalty.

"Sir, thank you and bless you for coming out on a terrible day like this. We're going to play this show for you as if the house were completely packed."

The old man replied, "Gee, thanks, but would you minding hurrying it up? I'm the janitor and I'd like to get home early."

11

He and She . . .

A man will stand for anything
Without a fight or fuss.
A man will stand for anything
Except a lady in a bus.

The girl had a dream, a beautiful dream. A handsome prince galloped up on a white horse and stopped right in front of her house. He jumped off his horse, dashed into the house and picked her up in his arms. Then he carried her out of the house, leaped into the saddle, holding her gently but strongly in his arms. The horse whirled about and raced swiftly away. Soon the town was behind them; ahead were beautiful meadows, hills and woodlands. In the distance stood his castle, high on a mountain. It was a beautiful castle with a rainbow over it. They galloped up to it. He carried her inside and into a beautiful room. Colorful tapestries hung on the walls and a fire was crackling in a huge fireplace. Taking her hand, the prince led her up a graceful stairway to a delightful room all decorated with laces, satins and ribbons, gently perfumed, and sat her on a white mink sofa.

She was trembling; she had never been so thrilled before. "Now what are you going to do with me?" she asked.

The prince shook his head. "How should I know. It's your dream."

The very, very wealthy girl was being courted by a persistent young man. "My little honeysuckle," he said, "My Rocky Mountain wildflower. Of course you are a very wealthy girl, aren't you?"

"I am. I'm worth a million and a quarter, last time I looked at my bank accounts. And how much are you worth?"

"Last time I looked into my pocket, it was seven dollars and nineteen cents."

"And you are in love with me?"

"Oh, desperately," he said.

"Why?"

"For your money, of course."

"Oh, I see."

"I hope I'm not out of line," he said. "But I have something to ask you . . . Will you marry me?

She said, "No."

"I didn't think you would."

"Well, if you didn't think I would, why did you ask me?"

"I wanted to know how a man feels when he loses a million and a quarter dollars."

> Her eyes were bright and shining;
> Her skin was soft as rain.
> She stole my heart; she stole my soul,
> My wallet, watch and chain.

She fell in love with the butcher because she always played for big steaks.

A traveling salesman was trying to sleep in an upper berth on a train. There was a rather persistant tapping on his bed, and this old spinster kept saying, "Mr. Collins, oh Mr. Collins." "Yes, what is it?" "Mr. Collins, it's frightfully cold down here. Would you mind getting me another blanket?" "Lady, I'll tell you what. I've got a wonderful idea. Let's pretend we're married." She giggled shyly. "Oh, I think that would be very nice." "Good, now go get your own blanket."

The young man brought his girl home early. Then he knocked on the door of her father's room. "Mr. Lampok," he said, "may I see you for a minute?" "Come in, young man, come in." "Sir, I . . . I . . . don't really know how to ask you this . . ." "Not another word, son. I pride myself on being a good judge of character. I want my little girl to be happy. So, of course, you have my permission." "What permission?" "Permission to marry my daughter." "I don't want to marry your daughter. I'm behind fifty dollars on my car payments, and I was wondering . . ." "Get out of here! I hardly know you, you bum!'

> There was a young lady named Stella
> Fell in love with a bow-legged fella.
> The venturesome chap
> Let her sit on his lap,
> And she plummeted down to the cellar.

"She Was Only a Printer's Daughter, but She Certainly Was the Type."

Two old darlings were talking about marriage. Both had recently remarried. "How's everything going with the new hubby?" "I don't want to talk about it." "What sort of marriage have you got? I mean, my marriage is sort of a cultural marriage, not a lot of sex, but we go for long walks, we visit museums and we see art. Now what sort is yours?" "I guess you could say that I've got what they call an agriculture marriage." "What's that?" "I wish my old man was six feet under and he wishes I was six feet under."

The two men were talking about women, and one said, "You know, I really don't understand the way women's minds work. A woman will go out and spend fifty dollars for a bathing suit, put it on, go to the beach, and never go in the water." The other man said, "Yes, women are funny. But one thing I do know. When a woman puts on a bathing suit, she may never go into the water. And when a woman puts on a riding habit she may never go horseback riding. But when a woman puts on a bridal gown, she means business."

Two Frenchmen, François and Maurice, had an argument over Marie. Finally Maurice took his glove and slapped François on the face and said, "I will meet you on the field of honor tomorrow morning. There we will continue our argument with pistols. Be there at six o'clock." The next morning at six o'clock François was there. All of a sudden a messenger ran up and handed him a note: "Dear F., I am on my honeymoon with Marie. Start by yourself."

A young couple, much in love, were walking along the beach, arm in arm, on a beautiful night. And the young man just waxed poetic for a moment: "Roll on, thou deep and dark blue ocean. Roll on." And the girl gazed at the breakers for a moment, and in hushed and reverent tones she said, "Oh, Herman, you wonderful man. It's doing it. It's doing it."

One farmer walked up to another and said, "Look here, Mulvane, you've heard of the Widow Johnson?" "Oh yes, that young thing that lives up on the hill." "Yup, that's the Widow Johnson. She's only twenty-eight years old and her husband left her penniless. Well, we at the church are having a raffle for the Widow Johnson. Wouldn't you like to buy a ticket?" "Well, I wouldn't mind buying a ticket; but if I won her, my wife wouldn't let me keep her no way."

> The shades of night were falling fast
> When for a kiss he asked her.
> She must have answered yes
> Because the shades came down much faster.

A young man ran into a minister's house. "Please, please, Reverend, I've got this beautiful girl here, and you've got to marry us. Please, I've got the license, I've got the blood test, I've got two dollars, and those two ladies sitting over there in the corner will be fine as witnesses. Please, sir, please." The minister agreed to perform the ceremony, but he felt he had to remind the couple, "Don't forget the old adage about marrying in haste." The groom protested, "We can't wait. We're double-parked."

Slim was a steady hanger-on at the poolroom. The little man who ran the store next door was a born matchmaker, and he was always after Slim to get married. "Hey, man, what are you going to do? Shoot pool for the rest of your life? It's time you settled down, got a steady job and married a good girl. You get married and it'll change the whole perspective on your life."

"Look, baby, there ain't but one woman in the world for me . . . She's got to be about five two, have a face like a movie star, the figure of a Miss America, a great personality, like to play pool, and have as much money as a Rockefeller. That's the only gal I am going to marry."

"Now, Slim, be reasonable. Look at yourself. You aren't even good-looking. You don't know anything but shooting pool. You don't have a job. . . . You'd be lucky to get any kind of wife. A chick like you want would have to be crazy to marry you."

"I don't care if she's crazy . . . so long as she has all those other qualifications."

Song Title: "Some Girls Like to Be Kept in Suspense, Others Prefer Apartments."

An old maid rushed into a police station, crying, "Oh, I was walking in the park and a man threw his arms around me and embraced me passionately and he kissed me and he kissed me and he kissed me." The cop asked, "When did this incident take place?" "Oh, about 23 years ago this September." "You can't expect us to arrest a man for something he did 23 years ago." "I don't want you to arrest him. I just love talking about it."

A wealthy man was in love with a chorus girl. He told her, "I cannot live without you." She said, "What are you, putting me on or something?" "Oh, no! I have watched you from afar and I tremble when I see you walk upon the stage. I want you to be mine." She said, "Listen, I'm not cheap, you know. If you want me to be yours, I'll want furs, jewelry, a car, a nice apartment." "Whatever is your pleasure, I shall give it to you." And he poured $20,000 in gifts upon her in two months. He came up one day with a huge diamond ring. He said, "My love, my treasure, my lotus blossom, my goodness . . . I would like you to become my wife." "Are you kidding? You think I'd marry you, the way you throw your money around?"

There was maid with such graces
That her curves cried aloud for embraces.
"You look," said a he, "like a million to me,
Invested in all the right places."

A blues song?: "I Am Always Chasing Rainbows, Because I Can't Seem to Find Any Girls."

Adam had been roaming through the Garden of Eden all alone for quite a while. The Lord knew man could not live alone, so He put Adam to sleep, took out a rib and from it created Eve. Adam married her and they lived happily in the Garden of Eden. One night, he came home late. The next night he came home later. Eve was furious. "You're not true to me. There's another woman." Adam protested, "There's no other woman. Here, count my ribs."

This was found in the diary kept by a young lady crossing the ocean for the first time. "Monday: I feel highly honored to be sitting at the captain's table. Tuesday: I spent the morning on the bridge with the captain. I think he likes me. Wednesday: The captain made indecent proposals, unbecoming an officer and a gentleman. Thursday: The captain threatened to sink the ship if I did not comply with his romantic proposals. Friday: I saved 600 lives."

Dear Editor: Two weeks ago, I caught my wife kissing John. Last week it was Phil; this morning it was Bill. What should I do? Signed, Worried."

Dear Worried: Cheer up, your turn will come.

Three marvelous old maids who had been out on the town returned home to find their house had been ransacked. One old maid looked around and she said, "Girls, be careful. The burgler could still be in the house. We'd better check out our bedrooms before we go to sleep. So let's go upstairs." They went upstairs. The first old maid went to her room and said, "He's not here." The second old maid went to her room and looked, "Nobody here." The third old maid said, "Goodnight, girls."

Another song: "I Always See Her in My Dreams, That's Why I Stay Awake."

A beautiful lady was sitting at a bar. A man walked over and said, *"Pardonez-moi.* I was sitting over there when I saw you walk in. The light flickering through your hair and that white fur against your soft pink skin made me realize that I have never before seen anyone as beautiful as you." She just looked at him. "I'd like to lay Manhattan at your feet, and cover you in jewels and furs. I'd take you to Paris, Rome, and finally to Egypt for a moonlight trip down the Nile. Would you like to come?" She said, "Yes, I would love to come." "Here's my card. Go home and prepare yourself, my Juliet, and then my Rolls Royce will come and get you and we will fly away in my private plane." She said, "Is this your town telephone number or the number of your country estate?" "Actually it's the delicatessen downstairs, but they'll call me."

Two girl friends met and one said to the other, "I hear you broke your engagement?" "That's right." "But you said that you were going to marry him because he was so rich. That's all that mattered to you, that he had a lot of money. What happened?" "Well, one day I saw him in a bathing suit and, without a wallet, he looked like a slob."

An alarm was phoned into the fire-house. Twenty firemen

jumped into the truck, rushed out to the address, ran up the stairs and hammered on the door. An old maid answered the door. "Where's the fire?" the chief shouted. "I've got twenty firemen here. And there seems to be no fire!" "That's right. Nineteen of you can go back."

A salesman was traveling through the back country one night when his headlights went out. He walked back to the farmhouse he remembered passing and knocked on the door. He told the farmer: "The headlights on my car have gone out. I'd like to stay the night. In the morning in the daylight I can drive into town to a garage." The farmer agreed to let him stay and took him upstairs to a bedroom. Just as the salesman was dozing off, he heard a knock on the door and a girl's voice asking, "Are you awake?" He said he was. "Would you mind company?" He assured her he would love company. She said, "Here's another salesman without headlights."

Two girls were talking and one sighed, "Oh, Charles! Charles is so marvelous. He spoils me. He takes me every place in a taxi." "Everyone says he must be rich."

"No, he's a taxi driver."

Song titles:

She Was Only a Moonshiner's Daughter, But I Love Her Still.

I Call My Girl Muscles, Because She's in Everybody's Arms.

I Call My Girl Toothpaste, Because I Like to Squeeze Her in the Middle.

A lady just past her prime walked into a Chinese Restaurant and ordered a meal. "I'll have some Egg Drop soup, a plate of Chow Mein and . . . and . . . that's all." "Would you like some rice?" the waiter asked. "Thrown at me, dearie, thrown at me."

Joyfully, the woman reread the letter from her daughter

who had been living abroad. The daughter wrote that she
had found and married just the kind of man her mother had
been telling her to marry. And would she come to visit the
newly wed couple. Of course the woman reserved a seat on
the very next plane to Africa. There she joined a safari going
into the most remote part of the jungle. It took her over a
week to get to the village where her daughter was living.
There in the middle of the compound she saw her girl. Next
to her, all rigged out in feathers, leopard skin, a hideous
headdress, and with a bone thrust through his nose, stood
the tribe witch doctor. Her daughter waved and ran to her,
and as they hugged, the mother whispered to her daughter:
"But, darling, you misunderstood. Mama always said 'rich
doctor.' "

As soon as the man checked out of his hotel room, it was
rented to a newly married couple. About fifteen minutes
later the man rushed back into the hotel and explained to
the clerk that he had forgotten his umbrella in the room.
The clerk told him he could go up to get it but that he would
have to knock on the door because it was already occupied.
The man went up and just as he was about to knock on the
door he heard a voice inside saying, "Oh, darling, whose
beautiful golden hair is that?"

A woman answered, "Yours, sweetheart."

"And whose pretty little nose is that?"

"Yours, sweetheart."

"And whose gorgeous ruby lips are those?"

"Yours, forever, dear."

The man quickly opened the door and called out, "When
you get to the black umbrella—it's mine."

One old maid said to another, "At the dances every year,
I used to love it as a young girl. Oh, I was lovely. I was
squired by the best of men. Ah, memories! How I remember
—moonlight, cornsilk, the gay life. And may I say that I
have been asked to be married many times." "By whom?"
"By my mother and father."

A woman who was going through her husband's pockets because she wanted to send the suit to the cleaners found a little piece of paper on which was written: "Belle Brown, Tremont 2012." She waited for him to get home from work, then asked him what the name and number meant. He said, "Darling, why are you so suspicious? You know I play the horses. This is the name of the horse, and Tremont is the code name for the bookie and the odds were 2012." His wife apologized. "I'm sorry I mistrusted you." Just then the phone rang. She picked it up and said, "Hello." She listened, then put the receiver down on the table, and said, "It's your horse. She wants to speak to you."

An oversize woman trying to get into a bus got stuck in the door. She couldn't get in and she couldn't get out. She turned to the gentleman behind her and said, "If you were half a man, you'd give me a hand." He said, "If you were half a woman, you wouldn't need any."

Love song: "I Call My Girl 'Keyhole,' Because She's Something to Adore."

A traveling salesman came home after a week's trip. As he was telling his wife all about the trip, the telephone rang. He picked it up. "Hello. Yes? What? I don't know." He hung up. His wife asked, "Who was it?" "Some man who must think we live on the beach—he wanted to know if the coast was clear."

A young fellow had been visiting his girl, and they had had a lovely evening, but now it was time to go home. Just then her father walked in and said, "Young man, you can't go home in weather like this. It's pouring out there, and it's the worst rainstorm we've had in years. You'd better stay here." "Oh, thank you very much." The girl went in to speak to her mother and her father went back to his den. When she came back into the parlor, her boy friend was gone. Everyone looked around and couldn't find him. About half an hour later, the doorbell rang and, when they opened the door, there stood the young man, soaking wet. "You were so nice to ask me to stay over, I ran home to get my pajamas."

A mouse in her room woke Miss Dowd
And she was frightened, it must be allowed.
Soon a happy thought hit her:
To scare off the critter
She sat up in the bed and meowed.

*A rich variety of exciting and enjoyable
reading in Tempo Books—*

SPORTS

4879. MY GREATEST DAY IN BASEBALL   75¢

John P. Carmichael and other noted sports writers. This is a sports book
that's different. Here a reader can find out how the player himself felt
about his own *Greatest Day in Baseball*. And what days they were!
Koufax pitching his fourth no-hitter . . . Yastrzemski's hitting rampage
in the last game of the 1967 season . . . Ruth's historic home run in the
1932 World Series . . . all are here, and many more. Thirty-six great
stories told by and about today's top stars and the all-time greats of baseball history. A book that will be read over and over and over again.

4877. DAREDEVILS OF THE SPEEDWAY   75¢

Ross Olney. The roar of the mighty engines . . . the smell of burning fuel
. . . the constant tension . . . the high speeds . . . and the checkered
flag—that is the breakneck daredevil game of auto racing. This history
of the Indianapolis "500" contains true life-and-death stories of its most
famous drivers.

5337. WILLIE MAYS   75¢

Arnold Hano. (revised edition) Starting from afternoon ball-catching
sessions with his father—at age 3—right through the past season when he
hit his 600th home run, this book is the complete story of Willie. It
dramatically tells the ups and downs of his career as he rose to the top
of his trade in the professional leagues.

4897. THE JOHNNY UNITAS STORY   75¢

Johnny Unitas and Ed Fitzgerald. The amazing personal account of how
a hard luck kid who wouldn't quit became a star quarterback and the
most phenomenal passer in pro football history. Telling about his colorful,
exciting life in football, the passing wizard of the Baltimore Colts blends
his personal story with his own keen analysis of football strategy and
execution.

4888. RUN TO DAYLIGHT!   75¢

Vince Lombardi. The thrilling, behind-the-scenes drama of pro football,
told by the greatest coach in the history of the game. Only Vince
Lombardi, the fiery, dynamic leader of the champion Green Bay Packers
—knows what it's really like to guide a team of world champions through
the grueling schedule of a professional football season.

4862. THE MAKING OF A PRO QUARTERBACK   50¢

Ed Richter. Here is probably the most authentic book ever written on
professional football. From training camp to championship game, it tells
how quarterbacks learn their trade and play the game.
". . . much useful information."—The New York Times

5340. THE AMAZING METS   75¢

Jerry Mitchell. (revised edition) Jerry Mitchell, sportswriter for the
New York Post, and cartoonist, Willard Mullin, combine their talents to
tell the truth-is-funnier-than fiction story of baseball's Cinderella team.
The record breaking 21-game losing streak. . . the 23-inning loss to the
San Francisco Giants . . . the 1969 World Series . . . here is the whole,
wacky, wonderful story of the New York Mets and their cheering, ever-
faithful fans.

ADVENTURE

5325. FIRST ON THE MOON 75¢
Hugh Walters. The U.S. rocket Columbus and the Russian rocket Lenin are hurtling toward the moon, each carrying a human passenger intent on making the first landing on its surface.

4871. Rod Serling's TWILIGHT ZONE REVISITED 60¢
Edited by Walter Gibson. By the Emmy Award-winning TV writer, a collection of chilling stories.
Readers will share the terror of a young army officer cursed with the ability to see the glow of death on the faces of men about to die; they will fight under Custer in the battle of the Little Big Horn and marvel at those who miraculously survived—or did they?

5354. MINDS UNLEASHED 95¢
Edited by Groff Conklin. The power and the possibilities of the human mind—as uncharted as deep space—are explored in this collection of science fiction stories by masters of imagination, Isaac Asimov, Robert Heinlein, Arthur C. Clarke, Murray Leinster, Poul Anderson and others expand the limits of the mind and suggest some of the dramatic potentialities of the future.

5356. PLANETS FOR SALE 75¢
A. E. Van Vogt and E. Mayne Hull. In this future world, space travel is a commonplace and business tycoons scramble for advantage on far-flung planets. The action is in the Ridge Stars, a pioneer galaxy as yet uncontrolled by anyone, and the attempts of billionaire Arthur Blord to seize control.

5313. GREAT STORIES OF SPACE TRAVEL 60¢
Groff Conklin. Who knows what strange things will confront those brave Earthlings in the years to come who dare to invade the far reaches of outer space . . . and beyond?
In these stories, a group of science fiction's greatest writers (Isaac Asimov, Ray Bradbury, A. E. Van Vogt, and others) speculate on the nature of those dangers.

5306. ATTACK FROM ATLANTIS 75¢
Lester del Rey. Here is a suspense-filled tale of underwater adventure written by one of America's most honored science fiction writers. In this intriguing tale, Lester del Rey writes of an outcast race that has migrated into the sea and of a young boy who tries to escape from "the city of no return."

5344. VOYAGERS IN TIME 95¢
Edited by Robert Silverberg. A collection of twelve science fiction stories about time travel by such authors as H. G. Wells, Lester del Rey, Poul Anderson and others. Exciting, challenging accounts of voyages back and forward in time—their complexities and hazardous consequences.

4709. MYSTERY OF SATELLITE 7 50¢
Charles Coombs. When Argus 7 mysteriously explodes at an altitude of 42 miles, talk of sabotage runs loud. And suddenly three young people are catapulted from their role of privileged observers to land square in the center of the satellite mystery.

5359. THE WEAPON MAKERS 75¢
A. E. Van Vogt. One of the all-time great science fiction novels by one of the great masters. A psychological suspense novel about a man whose secret is that he is immortal and whose goal is to save the world when the weapon makers forget that they are sworn to preserve peace and attempt to take over the entire universe.

CLASSICS

4867. THE JUNGLE BOOK   50¢
Rudyard Kipling. Saved from the snatching jaws of Shere Khan, Mowgli is raised by Mother Wolf as one of her own cubs. The full original text.

5322. PENROD   75¢
Booth Tarkington. This is the only inexpensive edition of the classic which has delighted and inspired mischief-lovers for years. The story of Penrod Schofield is the story of all high-spirited American boys. Stirring up fun for himself and his friends, and trouble for his enemies and elders, Penrod does all the things that boys have always done, but somehow they turn out funnier.

4755. DADDY-LONG-LEGS   60¢
Jean Webster. A girl grows to young womanhood in an orphanage, and is sent to college by an unknown benefactor. This gay, tender, whimsical record of Judy's correspondence with her mysterious guardian has enchanted readers of all ages since it was first published. It has been translated into eighteen languages, and filmed twice, most recently with Leslie Caron and Fred Astaire playing the leading roles.

5341. DEAR ENEMY   75¢
Jean Webster. This sequel to *Daddy-Long-Legs* follows in the same engaging tradition of delightful romance. It's all here, the timeless appeal, humor and youthful wisdom that endeared Jean Webster's first youngster to millions of readers and to her now famous Daddy-Long-Legs.

4761. A LANTERN IN HER HAND   60¢
Bess Streeter Aldrich. Abbie Deal, brought up in a log cabin in Iowa, took the covered wagon trail to Nebraska as a young bride. In a rude shelter on the prairie she raised her family and stood beside her husband through all the heartbreaking struggles of the pioneer days—and became part of an epic.

5304. ANNE OF GREEN GABLES   75¢
Lucy M. Montgomery. The only unabridged reprint available. Red-headed, dreamy Anne, the orphan who brings happiness and love into the lives of her foster parents, is one of the most beloved heroines in all literature. Millions of girls throughout the world have taken her to their hearts.

4795. PETER PAN   60¢
James M. Barrie. The only inexpensive paperback version of this delightful fantasy—the classic story of Peter and Wendy and the amazing adventures that befall them in Never-Never-Land.

4763. REBECCA OF SUNNYBROOK FARM   75¢
Kate Douglas Wiggin. Living with her maiden aunts would doubtless be "the making of Rebecca" everybody thought, so the little girl with the enormous eyes and most remarkable talent for mischief was shipped to a house where children were supposed to be seen and not heard. Yet nothing could dampen Rebecca's lively spirits, and nobody could resist her winsome charm.

4841. WIND IN THE WILLOWS   60¢
Kenneth Grahame. If a poll were taken of the book best loved by boys and girls over the generations, the winner hands down, would most likely be this one. This enchanting book, packed with the adventures of Mole, Rat, Toad and their friends, is the kind of story that keeps children spellbound. Illustrated.